Temples and Sanctuaries
of Ancient Greece

The Athenian Acropolis seen from the south.

Temples and Sanctuaries of Ancient Greece

A Companion Guide

Edited by EVI MELAS

with 117 illustrations, 29 in colour

THAMES AND HUDSON · LONDON

Translated from the German *Tempel und Stätten der Götter Griechenlands*
by F. Maxwell Brownjohn

© 1970 Verlag M. DuMont Schauberg, Cologne
English translation © 1973 Thames and Hudson Ltd, London

Printed in Switzerland by Roto Sadag, Geneva

ISBN   0 500 25035 9 *clothbound*
       0 500 27024 4 *paperbound*

Contents

The ancient centres discussed in individual essays are treated by geographical groupings:

1) MAINLAND (including Peloponnese), accessible from Athens: Amphiareion; Argos; Brauron; Delphi; Eleusis; Epidaurus; Olympia; Mt Ptoion; Rhamnus; Sparta

2) MAINLAND (Epirus): the Oracle of the Dead on the Acheron; Dodona

3) AEGEAN ISLANDS: Delos; Samos; Samothrace

A brief note on methods of reaching each site appears on pp. 203-206.

Foreword

This book is intended as a guide to the significance and importance of some of the principal sanctuaries of ancient Greece. Drawing on myth, historical evidence and architectural remains, it seeks to convey the powerful living spirit which even today emanates from these places of worship. The reader who is sensible of his ties with humanist and philhellenic tradition may derive a singular fascination from the authors' explanatory comments on Hellenic sanctuaries, many of which may already be known to him and some of which he may have visited or be hoping to visit in the near future.

The individual contributors are experts, most of whom can lay claim to important publications which have earned them international repute in the field of archaeology. Some have been principally responsible for exploring the sanctuaries they write about or owe their exhaustive knowledge to long years of official activity as curators. J. TRAVLOS, who has worked at Eleusis for many years and is a leading authority on Greek architecture, played a major part in research on the early history of the sanctuary, just as S. DAKARIS helped to excavate Dodona and evaluate the finds made there. Dakaris was also responsible for discovering and excavating the Oracle of the Dead beside the Acheron, which has shed an entirely new light on the death-cult of the ancients and is unique among sanctuaries known to us. J. KONDIS, for some years a government commissioner, has collaborated with German archaeologists at Olympia, and his own research has given him a thorough grounding in the topographical and historical problems associated with this pan-Hellenic festival site. Kondis has also published a substantial work on the sanctuary of Artemis at Brauron, which forms the subject of his second contribution to this book. The excavation of this sanctuary on the east coast of Attica, one of the most important discoveries made on

Greek soil during the 1950s, was also in part the work of IOANNIS PAPADIMITRIOU, the Greek archaelogist who before his untimely death played a major part in reorganizing the preservation of ancient monuments in Greece. As Director of the Acropolis Museum in Athens, G. DONTAS is now responsible for the site where he once worked as a budding scholar. A. DELIVORRIAS held an official post at Sparta before moving to the Institute of Archaeology at Tübingen University. Those contributions which are less intimately connected with their authors' specialized field of research are none the less based on abundant knowledge, and are written with perceptive affection and enthusiasm for Greek antiquity.

The authors include those who, having grown up during the Second World War and the domestic turmoil which subsided only in the early 1950s, received their professional training under extremely adverse conditions, and some young scholars who were able to pursue and complete their studies in much more propitious circumstances, and have travelled widely to augment their studies. Only two of the authors are representative of the generation which had already won its academic spurs before the outbreak of war. The oldest contributor is PANAYOTIS KANELLOPOULOS, a former prime minister of Greece. Kanellopoulos, though not a professional archaeologist, has remained a scholar and historian since his student days at Heidelberg, and even after abandoning his teaching activities at Athens University in favour of politics. His concluding essay on the concept of sanctity and religious beliefs among the Hellenes summarizes, from a more general viewpoint, the particular images conjured up by the essays on individual sanctuaries.

To the best of my knowledge, the present collection of essays is the first in which Greek archaeologists have addressed themselves to a wide readership through this medium. They speak of relics which, preserved by their native soil, form part of an environment familiar to them from childhood. The discerning reader will derive much more from this book than the authoritative information about *ancient* Greece of which its title gives promise.

EMIL KUNZE

Athens : the Acropolis

The sun-drenched plain of Athens lies between the mountains and the sea, fringed by gently undulating hills. From its centre rises a bare, rugged rock which, millennia before the monuments of the Acropolis or citadel as we know it, developed, had provided shelter in Neolithic times. The rock seemed naturally suited to habitation and defence: not only was it accessible from one side only, but it afforded sufficient space for the few early inhabitants and supplied them with pure spring-water. When, towards the close of the Mycenaean period, *c.* 1100 BC, this stronghold was gravely menaced by Dorian invaders, it was enclosed with massive stone walls – the remains of which can still be seen today.

The royal palace was situated on the north side of the plateau beside a secret stair cut into the rock. Inside this royal abode the major deities of the Mycenaean world were worshipped with impressive ceremony: the all-powerful goddess of nature and fertility and her cult-partner, a lesser god who consorted with her in three roles, as child, lover and mortal husband. This, too, was where the king himself received divine honours, both during his lifetime and after his death, and hence his residence became a sanctuary. When the kingship was abolished in Athens at the close of the Mycenaean period and the centre of the city was displaced from the confines of the Acropolis, the deserted palace remained a holy place. Little by little, the sacred precinct came to encompass the whole of the rocky plateau.

Towards the end of the Geometric period, *c.* 750–700 BC, the pantheon of Olympian gods, demigods, daemons (spirits) and heroes crystallized out of the wealth of traditions that stemmed from Mycenaean prehistory and the early centuries of the historical era. The Greek myths were rooted partly in religious tradition and rites of the past, partly in historical events that had been dramatized or distorted by the passage of

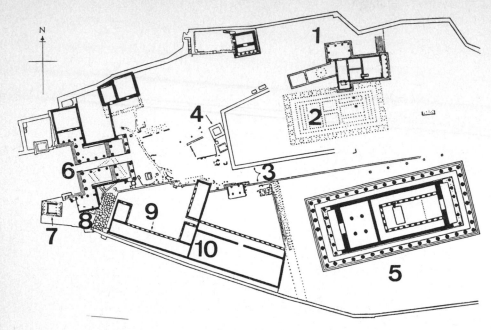

Plan of the Acropolis: 1, Erechtheum; 2, Old Temple of Athena; 3, terrace walls; 4, site of statue of Athena Promachos by Phidias; 5, Parthenon; 6, Propylaea; 7, Temple of Athena Nike; 8, Mycenaean walls; 9, sanctuary of Artemis Brauronia; 10, Chalkotheke.

The Mycenaean wall, with the west end of the Parthenon beyond.

time. For example, the mythical King Cecrops loomed large in the minds of the Athenians of the historical period, who were still taking their first tentative steps on the road to civilization. They believed that it was he who had divided Attica into communities (demes), introduced monogamy, raised the first altar to Zeus, consecrated the first statue to the goddess Athena, and substituted the fruit of the soil for sacrificial slaughter. This last act, in particular, provides sufficient proof that Cecrops was the successor of some prehistoric earth-dwelling deity. The Athenian conception of his appearance – a man shaped like a serpent below the waist – is another pointer to his origin. We know that the snake symbolized the forces of the earth, so the Athenians evidently believed Cecrops to be a son of the earth.

A pre-eminent place in the complex domain of faith and worship in historic Athens was reserved for the goddess Athena: she was regarded as the tutelary goddess and protector of the city. Tradition had it that she sprang, armed and helmeted, from the brow of her father Zeus. She was the Achaeans' martial helpmate during the Trojan War and also assisted other heroes such as Heracles. Another of her manifestations is less well known: like so many goddesses and demigoddesses, she was descended from a great prehistoric mother-goddess, and like them, she ruled the forces of the earth, protecting crops, harvests and mortal men. The cult of Athena's sacred serpent (kept in her temple on the Acropolis) dated back to prehistoric times, as did that of the owl – which Messenian refugees brought to Athens when the Dorians captured Pylos c. 1200 BC.

About 700 BC a small temple was erected on the Acropolis to house the goddess's first cult-statue. The brick walls and wooden framework disintegrated in the course of time, leaving only two stone bases that once supported wooden columns. These can now be seen in front of the Erechtheum. The olive-wood figure had, the Athenians believed, fallen from the sky. Written accounts and Archaic clay statuettes enable us to reconstruct its appearance: it showed Athena seated with a head-dress (*polos*) on her head and a bowl in her right hand. The Athenians swathed the figure in a woollen tunic (*peplos*) and hung it with ornaments. Once a year clothes and adornments were removed and the wooden idol was borne to the sea to be ritually cleansed and to preserve its powers. The day of the Plynteria (rites of purification) was held to be inauspicious for major activities, since it was thought that the impurity removed from the cult-statue would fill the air and bring disaster.

Prehistoric religious ideas gave prominence not only to the great goddess but also to the cult-partner associated with her. In Athens, his name – Erichthonius – suggested that he was an earth-deity. Often assuming the guise of a serpent, he dwelt in the temple of Athena on the Acropolis and acted as its custodian. Sculptors frequently represented Erichthonius as a snake, e.g. on the shield of the chryselephantine statue of Athena in the Parthenon. It is probable that Erechtheus was originally another name for the same deity. Homer says in the *Odyssey* that Athena forced her way into the house of Erechtheus, and speaks in the *Iliad* of Athena's resplendent temple. What is meant in both cases is the early temple of Erechtheus which, like its richly decorated classical successor, the Erechtheum, belonged jointly to Athena and Erechtheus. Erechtheus was later to be regarded as an historical figure, as king of Athens and father of King Pandion. The Athenians told how he vanquished and slew Poseidon's son, the Thracian King Eumolpus, who had joined forces with Eleusis against Athens. Erechtheus was thereupon slain, either by Poseidon with his trident or, at Poseidon's request, by Zeus with a thunderbolt.

According to the best-known Erechtheus myth, Athena was his mother. One tradition had it that she was the wife of Hephaestus, god of fire and of the arts, e.g. of the smith. Because the Athenians set store by their goddess's virginity, however, they sought to reconcile tradition with religious belief. Thus, Hephaestus failed to deflower his spouse, but his seed impregnated the earth and Gaea, the earth-goddess, conceived and bore Erichthonius/Erechtheus. Gaea gave the child to Athena to rear, and she – ashamed of what the other gods might say – laid the infant in a basket which she entrusted to the daughters of the Athenian King Cecrops with strict instructions not to open it and never to inspect its contents. The King's daughters, Aglauros, Herse and Pandrosos, covertly opened the basket and, driven mad by what they saw, leapt off the Acropolis. Traditions vary: one asserts that the little Erichthonius had a serpent's tail, another that he was lying there with a snake beside him, and yet another that the basket was empty save for two snakes. Suicide exalted the status of the princesses, who were still receiving divine honours in historical times. Aglauros was worshipped in a cave on the north-west slope of the Acropolis and Pandrosos in a sanctuary near Athena's olive tree beside the Erechtheum, while Herse had a festival, the Hersephoria, instituted in her honour. The names Herse and Pandrosos are related to the words for dew (*herse, drosos*). Evidently, the festival held near Athena's olive tree in the heat of summer was intended to conjure up the dew which would supply plants with moisture. The rites associated with this ancient festival may have been conducive to the survival of Herse and Pandrosos in myth (cults frequently led to the creation of myths in early times). On the other hand, it may be deemed more likely that the king's daughters helped to perpetuate the tradition of the great prehistoric goddess.

In June, the month of the so-called 'Scirophoria', a peculiar ceremony took place on the Acropolis. In the Arrhephorion, a building on the north side of the plateau, not far from the temple of Athena, were lodged virgins known as the Arrhephoroi (bearers of secret things). On the eve of the festival two virgins took a closed basket from the priestess of Athena. Neither the priestess nor the girls knew what it contained. The Arrhephoroi left the Acropolis by a secret exit, and at a given spot in the lower city exchanged the first basket for another, which they carried back to the Acropolis. We are told by a later commentator that the baskets contained 'snakes', phalli moulded out of dough, and pine branches. Comparison with religious customs observed by primitive tribes today suggests that these were symbolic fertility rites, and in particular shows how the ancient cult gave rise to the myth that Erichthonius was hidden in a basket and that the daughters of Cecrops were forbidden to look at him.

The best-known legend of all is associated with the northern part of the Acropolis and concerns the cult-signs left there by the gods in token of their presence: Athena's olive tree, the saline spring in the Erechtheum, and the indentation caused by Poseidon's trident. In the days of Cecrops, Athena and Poseidon contended for dominion over Attica. Poseidon's trident brought a salty spring gushing from the rock and Athena's spear caused an olive tree to sprout from the ground. Zeus resolved the dispute by summoning the gods to decide which gift was of greater value to the country, and Athena won the patronage of Attica by a single vote.

13

Reconstructions of the pediments of the Parthenon. The central subjects are: (east) the birth of the goddess Athena, and (west) Athena's struggle with Poseidon. Acropolis Museum. See p. 22.

The visible signs of this contest were the saline spring beneath the later Erechtheum and beside it, in the shrine of Pandrosos, the venerable olive tree. A few paces further east, at the summit of the rocky plateau, stood the great altar of Athena. There, as Homer himself says, the Athenians annually propitiated the goddess by sacrificing young men, bulls and lambs.

In the sixth century BC, during the time of the Pisistratids, the Athenians erected a big new temple, traces of whose walls can still be seen in front of the Erechtheum. The temple proper of Erechtheus consisted of two parts, each subdivided into three. One contained the wooden image of the goddess Athena and the other was devoted to the joint worship of Erechtheus and Poseidon. A colonnade ran round the entire building. Apart from its marble pediments, the temple was constructed of bluish limestone quarried on the Acropolis itself. The statues of the east pediment were over life-size and represented the battle between gods and giants. Some of these large figures, among them a magnificent Athena, can be seen in the Acropolis Museum.

This 'old temple of Athena' was destroyed in 480 BC by the Persians. (They also burnt the sacred olive, but the Athenians later claimed that it put forth a new shoot before the day was out.) Two years later the Athenians returned to their city, which they had evacuated before the Persian onslaught, and hastily built a wall round Athens and the Acropolis. They cleared the sanctuaries of rubble, assembled the smashed statues and votive offerings and concealed them among the rocks. The

Statue of Athena Parthenos;
Roman copy of the colossal 5th-
century BC figure sculpted by
Phidias for the new Parthenon.
National Museum, Athens.
See p. 21.

15

Head of Athena, from the old
Parthenon, 6th century BC. Acropolis
Museum, Athens.

'old temple' was provisionally repaired to receive the wooden image of
the goddess which had accompanied the Athenians into exile.

Pericles' ambitious building programme envisaged a structural complex designed to house all relics and cult-objects on the north side of the
Acropolis. The construction of this building, the Erechtheum, was
probably begun only later – during the Peace of Nicias (concluded in
421 BC), a breathing-space during the Peloponnesian War between Athens
and Sparta, which had exhausted the Athenians' energies.

The architectonic irregularities of the Erechtheum stem from its uneven
site and the endeavour to pay homage to cult-objects and heroes' graves
at one particular spot. As singular as the building itself, the cult associated
with it was that of the gods of the earth worshipped there. Bloody
sacrifices were made to the Olympian gods on altars beneath the open
sky, whereas sacrifices inside the Erechtheum, in the presence only of a
few initiates, did not entail slaughter.

Pausanias relates that no 'animate being' (*empsychon*) was sacrificed to Supreme Zeus (Hypatos), whose altar was situated beside the north colonnade of the Erechtheum, apparently because – despite his title – he was also an earth-god. His altar was quadrangular and had a recess to contain votive offerings. This recess was said to house the grave of Erechtheus, for it bore – and still bears – the marks of the trident with which Poseidon slew him, or, according to another tradition, of the thunderbolt which Zeus hurled at him. The vestibule of the Erechtheum gave on to a narrow two-storeyed chamber. On the lower level was the saline spring of Poseidon, which emitted murmurous sea-sounds when the wind blew from the south. Its name – 'the Sea of Erechtheus' – indicates that it was originally unconnected with Poseidon. (Other earthly deities, e.g. Demeter, also had a relationship with water.) The upper floor of the Erechtheum housed benches for participants in the arcane ceremonies which took place in the side chambers. No one was permitted to enter these chambers, which were regarded as sacrosanct; according to Pausanias, they contained altars to Poseidon (also used for sacrifices to Erechtheus), Hephaestus and the hero Butes.

The notion of joint sacrifice to Poseidon and Erechtheus on one and the same altar is in conflict with the tradition according to which the Athenian hero Erechtheus was slain by the pan-Hellenic god Poseidon. Nevertheless, both are related deities of prehistoric origin. Poseidon's name, together with the epithet – 'Earth-shaker' - which he already has in Homer, suggests that he is an earth-god. (It remains to be proved whether Erechtheus and Poseidon were originally a single deity who was later worshipped in two forms, or whether they were two gods who fought and were subsequently reconciled.) Hephaestus, to whom the second altar was dedicated, was also an earth-god and, according to one tradition, the father of Erechtheus just as the latter was the father or brother of Butes. Erechtheus' sovereign role and the similar character of the other cults account for the name given to this building: the 'temple' or 'house' of Erechtheus. Beside the west wall of the Erechtheum was the shrine of Pandrosos, and the sacred olive referred to above. (The olive tree to be seen there today was planted only two generations ago.)

An inscription dating from 409–408 BC states that the Cecropeum, or sanctuary of Cecrops, mythical ancestor of the Athenians, stood at the

The Erechtheum and tomb of Cecrops, with roof supported by caryatids.

south-west corner of the Erechtheum. Cecrops' tomb was situated beneath the pavement of the vestibule, whose roof was supported by caryatids (Korai).

The statue of Athena had its place in the eastern part of the Erechtheum. Beside it, according to Pausanias, stood a gold oil-lamp designed by the sculptor Callimachus which burned day and night but needed refilling only once a year. The lamp's bronze flue was fashioned like a palm frond.

However numerous the historical and religious relics in and around the Erechtheum, the southern part of the Acropolis owes its renown to that consummation of Greek art, the Parthenon. The Periclean Parthenon

The 5th-century Parthenon of Pericles, seen from the north-west.

which now stands on the Acropolis was not the first temple to occupy this site; it reposes on the foundations of an earlier Parthenon whose incomplete column-members were found embedded in the north wall of the Acropolis or distributed over the site. It remains to be proved conclusively whether work started on the earlier Parthenon after the Battle of Marathon and was abandoned at the time of the Persian invasion of 480 BC, or whether Cimon began it after the Persian Wars and building was discontinued when Cimon was ostracized. Inferences about the earlier building can be drawn from limestone fragments and an abundance of sculpture: two lions attacking a bull, a three-bodied daemon, Heracles in combat with the Triton (a merman, son of Poseidon), some large serpents, several panthers in low relief, and a running Gorgon. All these fragments are now in the Acropolis Museum.

The building of the first Parthenon, or 'proto-Parthenon', began in 566 BC, when the first Great Panathenaea were celebrated. The building was supposed to have measured 100 ft in length, hence Hekatompedon (the hundred-footed), a name which clung to the site after the temple's demolition and came to be applied to the cella (great hall) of the second Parthenon.

The proto-Parthenon housed a statue of Athena which differed greatly from the one in the later building. The Athenians were at pains to stress the warlike characteristics of their goddess. The statue represented her, not calmly seated but erect, youthful, belligerent, striding along in full armour with her spear raised. This is how she was depicted on Panathenaic amphorae (see p. 22) and the same pose recurs in Late Archaic bronzes found on the Acropolis. The people called her 'Athene Parthenos' (Virgin Athena). The great temple was probably demolished by the Athenians themselves to make room for a 'modern' building.

In the middle of the fifth century BC Pericles took charge of public affairs at Athens. Surrounded by such eminent figures as the sculptor

Painted decoration on a Panathenaic amphora showing Athena with spear and shield. British Museum, London.

◄ Three-bodied daemon, fragment from the old Parthenon, 6th century BC. Acropolis Museum, Athens.

Phidias, the philosopher Anaxagoras and his own mistress Aspasia, he mobilized the intellectual and artistic resources of his age and, with money from the goddess's treasury and that of his Delian allies, fulfilled at Athens and, more especially, on the Acropolis the grandest building programme in Greek antiquity.

The new Parthenon, built in the Doric style and enclosed by 8 × 17 columns, took shape in the centre of the rocky plateau on the foundations of the earlier and unfinished edifice. The creation of a gifted people and its artists, Phidias, Callicrates and Ictinus, it arose on the city's most hallowed site. The new chryselephantine statue of Athene Parthenos, 40 ft high and sculpted by Phidias, 'fashioner of gods', glittered at the back of the temple interior. The statue has not survived, but the National Museum at Athens possesses an unfinished copy known as the 'Athena

Lenormant'. This Athena was less warlike than the goddess in the old Hekatompedon. Quietly confident, she was the incomparable symbol of a wealthy maritime and commercial power whose influence extended far across the Hellenic world. The temple and its sculptural decoration were a hymn to the gods, with Athena at their head, to the city and the battles from which it had emerged triumphant.

The Parthenon was lavishly adorned with sculptures. The metopes were carved to represent the great martial pan-Hellenic myths: in the east the Gigantomachy (battle of Giants), in the south Lapiths battling with Centaurs, in the west Amazons, in the north the Trojan War. The frieze which ran round the interior of the temple gave a detailed account of the Panathenaic procession and the gods awaiting its arrival. Gods adorned the pediments (see p. 14), the central position in the east being allotted to the birth of Athena from the head of Zeus, an ancient theme enriched with new symbolism, while the west side, facing the entrance to the Acropolis, showed Athena and Poseidon contending for the mastery of Attica. Construction time – nine years plus a further six or seven for the production of sculptures – was surprisingly brief when one considers the technical problems involved, the Athenians' wide-ranging expansion in the east and south, and the phase of dynamic internal development through which they were currently passing.

The Panathenaea were not only the Athenians' most important festival but an event which reflected the prestige of the new city-state. Their history went back a long way: Erechtheus was reputed to have initiated them as 'Athenaea' only; Theseus reorganized them and, after he had combined the various Attic communities (demes) to form a city-state, he renamed them the 'Panathenaea'. Legend traces the festival back to prehistoric times, and the name 'Athenaea' indicates that it was originally a religious festival held in honour of the goddess Athena and devoid of the political significance which it acquired later. Pisistratus reconstituted the festivities and distinguished between the Great and Lesser Panathenaea. The Lesser were held annually, the Great every fourth summer in the month of Hekatombaeon. Pisistratus also added contests between singers and athletes. Victors were awarded Panathenaic amphorae, large jars containing oil from the goddess's olive trees. From the time of Pericles onwards, musical contests were added to the other events.

Detail of Panathenaic procession, from the Parthenon frieze: youths on horseback. 5th century BC. British Museum, London.

The climax of the Great Panathenaea came when, on the final day, the twenty-eighth of Hekatombaeon, the wooden figure of the goddess was presented with a new robe (*peplos*), the product of months of work on the Acropolis by two of the Arrhephoroi, known as the 'Ergastinae', who wove it and embroidered it with colourful designs representing the battle with the Giants, in which the goddess had distinguished herself. The presentation was attended by all inhabitants including metics (resident aliens).

The procession set off at sunrise from the Kerameikos (potters' quarter) with the *peplos* hoisted sail-fashion above a ship on wheels. It moved slowly through the city, via the Agora (market-place), to the Acropolis. In the lead walked young girls from prominent families, the Canephoroi (basket-bearers), who carried the utensils required for the great sacrifice. Then came the sacrificial beasts, cattle and sheep, followed by the Scaphephoroi, who carried bowls containing wax and sacrificial cakes, also water-carriers and branch-carriers (venerable old men with olive

23

Detail of east frieze from the Parthenon: Poseidon, Apollo and Artemis. 5th century BC. Acropolis Museum, Athens.

branches), senior officials, generals and envoys from other cities. Musicians, Athenian hoplites (heavily armed infantrymen) and charioteers completed the procession. At the Eleusinium, near the Agora, the procession halted. Attendants removed the *peplos* from its wagon and completed their journey to the Acropolis on foot.

It is not known how the goddess's statue was dressed. We only know that, for many centuries, the cult-statue to which the *peplos* was presented was the ancient and much-revered 'sky-fallen' wooden idol of Athena in the Erechtheum, not the chryselephantine statue by Phidias.

Animal sacrifice, to which Homer refers, formed the crux of the ceremony. In historical times, four cows and four sheep were slaughtered on the altar of Athena Hygieia, beside the Propylaea, and on the great altar of Athena Polias, sacrifice being made jointly to Athena and Pandrosos. Meat from the slaughtered beasts was given to government officials, whose share was determined by religious law, and the rest went to the people. Cows, too, were slaughtered in hecatombs (groups of a hundred); the finest cow in each group was presented to Athena Nike and the meat of the remainder distributed among the assembled crowd.

A small but important temple of Athena had been erected in ancient times on the Mycenaean wall near the entrance to the Acropolis. The figure of Athena became fused with that of the earth-goddess Nike, daughter of the Titan Pallas and of Styx, as Hesiod relates. In the sixth century BC, a tiny 'temple-dwelling' was erected for Athena Nike above the sacrificial pit. The goddess's wooden statue, substantially similar to that destroyed by the Persians, showed the goddess holding a helmet in her left hand and, in her right, the pomegranate which symbolized fertility and the blessings of peace. An inscription on the limestone altar in front of this temple states that it was dedicated by one Patrocles. Temple, sacrificial pit and altar were discovered shortly before the Second World War beneath the classical temple of Nike and may now be viewed there in a lower-lying vault which has been purposely left open.

Work on the sanctuary of Athena Nike, as on most of the sanctuaries on the Acropolis, was discontinued for years after the Persians' devastating incursion. The decree of 448 BC, which commissioned Callicrates, architect of the Parthenon, to build a new temple of Athena Nike, was not implemented until much later – probably during the Peace of Nicias.

The cult-statue of Athena Nike was described as *apteros* (wingless) because all other statues of Nike had wings (e.g. the Nike on the balustrade of the temple, and the Winged Victory of Samothrace.

Built against the south wall of the Acropolis, beside the Propylaea, was the sanctuary of Artemis Brauronia; Artemis was goddess of hunting and wild life, and of women in childbirth. This was an offshoot of the sanctuary at Brauron (cf. p. 49) on the east coast of Attica. Pisistratus, who came from Brauron, brought the cult of Artemis from there to the Acropolis in the sixth century BC, just as he also introduced Attica to other rustic cults – e.g. the cult of Dionysus from Eleutherae in Boeotia.

Cimon ordered the sanctuary of Artemis Brauronia on the Acropolis to be rebuilt after its destruction by the Persians. It acquired its final shape in the fourth century BC: two small temples, one for the old cult-statue and one for the new, a work by Praxiteles, linked by a colonnade (stoa) which ran along the wall.

25

Another sanctuary in the rocky citadel was sacred to Zeus Polieus (patron of the city) and had its origins in a remarkable cult. This sanctuary lay east of the Parthenon at the plateau's highest point. Its superstructure has entirely disappeared, and we owe our knowledge of its appearance to American archaeologists. Wheat and barley used to be sacrificed on the altar of Zeus; an ox approached and ate the votive offerings; one of the priests then killed it with an axe, threw the axe away and fled. Proceedings were then brought 'against the axe', which had either to be removed from within the city limits or cast into the sea. This ceremony was so old that it no longer rated as modern even in the fifth century BC. Traditionally thought to have been instituted by Erechtheus, it exemplifies the transition from 'fire-less' offerings of produce to bloody animal sacrifices.

Apart from the large official sanctuaries and temples, there were a number of less important ones: a shrine dedicated to Pandion, the remains of which are now displayed on the ground floor of the Acropolis Museum; another dedicated to Artemis Hecate, opposite the temple of

◄ The restored Temple of Athena
Nike on the Acropolis, 5th century BC.

Winged figure of Athena Nike,
from the temple balustrade,
5th century BC. Acropolis Museum,
Athens.

Nike; and, finally, the circular Ionic temple of Roma and of Augustus, which were erected east of the Parthenon during that emperor's lifetime.

'Attica was all festivals', wrote the sophist Maximus Tyrius in the second century AD. As time went by, more and more gods came to be worshipped in the clefts and caverns of the rocky Acropolis, which had ever been regarded as the abode of living spirits: Aglauros since ancient times in a cave on the north side of the plateau; Apollo and, later, Pan in some caves in the north-west; Aphrodite and her cult-partner Eros under the open sky in a sanctuary on the north-east slope. On the opposite side Dionysus, closely associated with festivals and with tragedy and comedy, during the sixth century BC, and was followed in the fifth century by Asclepius, god of medicine.

Turning one's back on the bustle of the modern metropolis of Athens and looking at the time-worn rocky plateau of the Acropolis, one is reminded of the words of the Greek poet Kafavis: 'Albeit we smashed their images, albeit we drove them from their temples, the gods live on.'

G. DONTAS

27

The orchestra and proscenium of the theatre, overlooking the 360-ft colonnade.

The Amphiareion

On the border between Attica and Boeotia, near Oropus, was established an oracular shrine dedicated to Amphiaraus. Here, over two thousand years ago, hypnotherapy was practised and the interpretation of dreams used as a form of therapy. Patients were entertained with plays, music, contests and festivals. Those undergoing treatment had to pay a special visitor's tax, and when recovered, they would make votive gifts – some of gold – indicative of their former afflictions. Other sufferers sought to bribe or exert pressure on the god by offering reproductions of their afflicted ears, hands or heads *before* undergoing successful treatment. This was not unusual by current moral standards; after all, the gods and heroes of the Homeric epics had shown the Greeks how effective a policy of give and take could be.

The Amphiareion is situated in a valley thirty miles from Athens; it was a favourite Athenian resort, especially from the third century BC onwards, when Oropus was subject to Athens politically. Before being ceded to the Athenians in 338 BC by Philip II of Macedon, it was the scene of frequent fighting between Boeotians, Athenians and Eretrians. Aristotle's pupils, the Peripatetics, would cover the distance from Athens in a single day; they found it an arduous trip but refreshed themselves at the numerous wayside hostelries which, as one of them wrote, 'offer an abundance of all that man needs for life and recreation'. In the days of the Roman Empire, under which the Amphiareion attained a new prime, Attic ephebes (young citizens) who used to walk the distance for training purposes were able to watch their fathers taking a cure at the other end. Fortified with wine and the contents of slave-borne picnic baskets, they relaxed in the shade of the pine-grove on the hill behind the theatre. Below them gleamed the marble of the proscenium and of the Hellenistic orchestra with five stone seats for priests. Further down, below a stepped terrace, stood the 360-ft long colonnade, and, parallel with that, a vast array of honorific statues: the Roman consul Lucius Cornelius Sulla and his wife Metella, Ptolemy IV of Egypt and his consort Arsinoë, priests, poets and politicians. Brutus, too, occupied a prominent position there, honoured by the Oropeans as a 'tyrannicide' after the murder of Julius Caesar. Today only the close-packed pedestals inscribed with names and particulars can be seen.

The Attic ephebes lazing in their pine-grove would also have been able to see the stadium below the colonnade, the baths and thermae, and – beyond the fast-flowing stream – the processional way, hotels catering for those accompanying the sick, wine-shops, workshops, the market-place, the custom-house, and numerous shops. Nothing can now be seen of the stadium, the site of which is occupied by a small museum, and the structural complex beyond the river was destroyed in the course of time. Temples and altars used to stand to the west of the sanctuary at the end of the valley, but remnants of the large sacrificial altar described by Pausanias and some upright columns dating from the early fourth century BC are all that meet the eye today. In the hall where patients practised incubation (i.e. sleeping in a holy place to obtain dreams from the gods), modern visitors can also inspect the uncomfortable 'pillows', or stone supports for the beds of the sick.

The local cult-legend represented Amphiaraus as the seer beloved of Zeus and Apollo who accompanied the celebrated Seven against Thebes in his capacity as a soothsayer. He predicted the downfall of the Seven but was himself spared from sharing their fate when Zeus cleft the ground with a thunderbolt so that Amphiaraus and his chariot were engulfed.

Mention of Amphiaraus' career is found in Argive tradition, which knew him as one of the earliest kings of Argos and husband of Eriphyle. Here, too, he was credited with powers of divination. Despite these, he failed to assess his wife's character correctly and granted her the right to arbitrate in any dispute that might arise between him and her brother Adrastus, second king of Argos. This arrangement led to disaster when Polynices, son of Oedipus, visited Argos to incite the Argives to war against Thebes and assert his claim to the throne of his native city by force. Adrastus was in favour of the expedition, Amphiaraus against it.

(a) Stone 'pillows' for the beds of the sick in the great hall; (b) One of the stone seats for the priests in the theatre; (c) The remains of the 360-ft hall in which incubation was practised; (d) Pedestals formerly supporting honorific statues.

Eriphyle was so tempted by the celebrated necklace which the gods of Olympus had given Polynices' great grandmother Harmonia, a daughter of Aphrodite, as a wedding gift, that she succumbed to bribery and brought about the war against Thebes. When he set out with the army of the Seven, Amphiaraus knew that the Argives would be annihilated by the Thebans. He divined that, by the will of Zeus, Adrastus would be spared for a second campaign, known as the campaign of the Epigoni, against Thebes, and that his sons would avenge Eriphyle's treachery. He may also have foreseen his own apotheosis. Disaster duly struck before the seven gates of Thebes. Only Adrastus returned to Argos on his winged charger Arion. During the final battle Zeus dispatched his eagle, which snatched Amphiaraus' spear in mid-air with its talons and dropped it at the spot where the seer was saved next day. This place, expressly marked out by Zeus, was claimed by the Thebans, the Euboeans and the people of Harma, who invoked an association between the name of their city and the chariot (*harma*) which carried Amphiaraus into the earth. The Thebans, who allegedly maintained a cult of Amphiaraus, asserted their right to the gold votive offering which Croesus, king of Lydia, had presented to Amphiaraus as a visitor's gift when he consulted the oracle. To quote Herodotus (VIII, 133–4), however: 'Thebans are not permitted to use the Oracle of Amphiaraus at all, because Amphiaraus once asked them to decide whether they would rather have him as an expounder of oracles or as an ally; both they could not have. They chose an alliance...'

Being a seer, Amphiaraus was transported *alive* 'to the outermost edge of the earth' – a euphemistic phrase for the kingdom of the dead – because only thus, from the underworld, could he function as a divine healer and soothsayer. Zeus preserved Amphiaraus from death and the permanent darkness of underworld existence, the fate to be expected by one smitten by the thunderbolt of divine wrath, and caused him to sink, still living, into the ground. This mark of divine favour also found expression in the name Amphiaraus (twice-holy) itself.

The contradictions in Amphiaraus' life-story – like the discrepancies which occur in other Greek myths and legends – indicate that from very ancient times it was part of the Greek character not to minimize or reconcile absolute opposites, but to allow them to exist side by side.

Detail of painted decoration on a Corinthian krater showing Amphiaraus setting out for the campaign against Thebes; on the left Eriphyle can be seen holding the necklace. See p. 30. Staatliche Museen, Berlin.

Amphiaraus owed his elevation from heroic to divine rank to the *Thebais*, the Homeric epic whose hero he was and from which he emerged as an immortal. In response to Homeric inspiration, the Oropeans established a cult of the god Amphiaraus and did their utmost to invest the Amphiareion with exclusive status.

The Amphiareion is assumed to have been founded at Oropus between 431 and 415 BC. Aristophanes certainly mentions it in 415 in a comedy of the same name. Until the fourth century BC the sanatorium of Amphiaraus did, in fact, enjoy a greater reputation than that of Epidaurus. Even the Persian general Mardonius, who clearly recognized the important bearing of oracular pronouncements on military tactics, set store by the oracle of Amphiaraus. On the eve of the great battles against the Greeks early in the fifth century BC he sent an emissary who managed by dint of bribery – 'barbarians' being granted access to certain oracles only – to practise incubation in the Amphiareion.

Even when, in times of moral decline, Athens sent envoys to obtain information through dreams about disputed land titles and similar problems, the oracle was not swamped with unduly trivial questions of the sort which predominated at other oracular shrines.

Where origin and personality are concerned, the difference between Asclepius, the god of medicine, and Amphiaraus lies in the trends of their therapeutic techniques. Asclepius, reared on Mount Pelion by the 'good Centaur' Chiron at his father Apollo's behest, emphasized the

33

curative powers of nature because Chiron had taught him a knowledge of herbs. Dreams were, of course, interpreted by his priests too, but Amphiaraus concentrated far more on the disrupted harmony between mind and body. The priests in the Amphiareion listened to accounts of dreams and recorded them, either on stone or by some other means. The resulting 'case histories' are said to have been a great help to Greek physicians, even under the Roman Empire.

On his arrival, the patient had his purse lightened by one drachma (later one-and-a-half). For this he received a rather weighty admission card consisting of a triangular bronze or elongated lead plaque stamped with the heads of Amphiaraus and Hygieia (the goddess of health).

Paragraph 6 of an excellently preserved inscription found in the Amphiareion, the *hieros kanon* – a sort of list of regulations dating from the period 420–350 BC – ordains that entrance fees must be paid in legal tender in full view of the janitor, whose presence was obligatory, doubtless because it deterred visitors from slipping counterfeit coins into the box.

The janitor had to inscribe the names and native cities of the prospective 'sleepers' on a wooden plaque to be publicly displayed – not as a visitors' book but as a form of check designed to exclude murderers and suspected criminals.

Ritual purification included the slaughter of a ram. Amphiaraus was not, however, as demanding as other gods. According to paragraphs 7 and 8 of the regulations, he permitted the sacrifice of swine and game as well, and made no distinction between black and white, male and female – indeed did not insist on 'perfection' in the sacrificial beast. The priest-cum-medical superintendent who conducted sacrificial rites during religious festivals undertook them on behalf of patients too, if he happened to be present in the sanctuary. Otherwise, devotees used to drive their sheep, swine or game to the Amphiareion themselves. Having slaughtered and dedicated them, they then sought out a place in the sacred grove where they prepared a meal after the manner of the Homeric heroes. Salt, bread and spit or cooking-pot were borrowed from the nearest farmhouse.

The *hieros kanon*, which can be seen at the local museum, informs us that during his one-year term of office the officiating priest was not

Votive relief: Archinus renders thanks to Amphiaraus (left) for the cure effected (right) by the sacred snake. First half of the 4th century BC. Archaeological Museum, Athens.

permitted to be absent 'for more than three consecutive days from the commencement of the great autumn rains to the ploughing season', and had to live in the sanctuary for 'at least ten days in every month'. The priesthood was held in such high esteem that the Oropeans dated decrees by the terms of office of their priests, who hailed from prosperous families. Honour apart, the post also involved more prosaic advantages – its incumbent received the shoulder-blade of every sacrificial animal.

The sacrificial altar unearthed by archaeologists matches Pausanias' description perfectly: 28 ft long by 14 ft wide, it ran north and south rather than east and west, which was previously considered to be the rule in Greece. It had a limestone foundation and consisted, as Pausanias said, of five members adorned with representations of various gods and heroes in addition to Amphiaraus, all of whom received their share of sacrifices. One relief, now in the National Museum, Athens, shows the sacrificial victim, and another the sleeping Archinus (first half of the fourth century BC), his swollen and afflicted shoulder being licked by serpents (right), while the same patient (left) renders thanks to the god for his cure. The sacred snakes kept in the Amphiareion – no rarity in ancient Greek sanctuaries – are ridiculed by Aristophanes: 'You [Amphiaraus] had better keep your snakes safely shut up in boxes, and stop selling quack remedies' (*Fragments*). In contrast to Aristophanes, veneration for Amphiaraus is clearly expressed by Homer, Pindar, Aeschylus, Sophocles and Euripides.

Pilgrims originally slept in the open, men to the east and women to the west of the altar. Later, incubation took place in the great colonnaded hall. This was enclosed by a portico with an inner row of 17 Ionic columns and an outer one of 41 Doric columns. Its walls were adorned with red and green meanders. In exceptional circumstances, incubation was also permitted in the temple's adyton (inner sanctum). In the central aisle, between Ionic columns, stood the large white cult-statue of Amphiaraus, which was still to be seen in Pausanias' day.

Few people cared whether Amphiaraus was a hero promoted to divine status or a god down-graded to the rank of hero. What mattered was that he performed miraculous cures over several centuries. The thighs of the statue were plastered by the faithful with waxed coins. The coins dropped off when the wax dried out and found their way into the temple treasury. Temple funds enjoyed a particular boom at the time of the *agones* (contests), which are first recorded in 335–334 BC. The autumn games celebrated in honour of Amphiaraus were held with great pomp, either annually or every fifth year. These Amphiaraea opened with a vigil (*pannychis*), which was followed by a festive procession, sacrifice, and various trials of skill on foot and horseback, involving walking, running, riding, unarmed combat, the spoken word and playing the cithara. Competitors from all over the known world – Athenians, Argives, Spartans, Romans, Asiatics, Sicilians, Macedonians – figure in the lists of victors and show that this aspect of the sanctuary's activities was not without importance. Reliefs illustrate the *apobasis*, a special type of contest in which athletes in full armour had to leap from a fast-moving chariot, overhaul it and leap back again. One of the *apobasis* reliefs was long construed by scholars as a portrayal of the Amphiaraus legend.

They failed to associate the scene with a contest and took it to represent rather Amphiaraus driving his chariot into the cleft riven in the ground by Zeus.

Quite apart from entrance, incubation and expiation fees, the Amphiareion's income included the earnings of numerous hostelries. Not only was wine reputed to have a comforting effect on those who had fasted, but the priests prescribed it liberally – in certain cases, at least – as a 'soporific medicine' of signal merit.

The Amphiareion was also renowned for its cool, pure water, particularly beneficial to those afflicted with disorders of the stomach, kidneys and bladder. The faithful were not, however, permitted to draw water from the spring beside the altar. Pausanias states that departing visitors used to toss gold or silver coins into it. The spring was taboo, for it was there that Amphiaraus had emerged from the gloom of the underworld to take possession of his dream-oracle. Philostratus, a sophist from Lemnos who lived at the time of Marcus Aurelius, describes an ancient painting thus (*Eikones*, xvi): 'Amphiaraus is depicted with his chariot, near his future sanctuary, driving into the cleft opened by Zeus. The helmet has fallen from his head his countenance is no longer that of a warrior but already that of a prophet who dedicates himself to Apollo . . . Apart from him, one sees the following allegorical figures: Oropus as a youth, the Sea as a blue-clad female figure, Truth in a white robe, the Dream clad in black and white because he rules over day and night. The cornucopia in his hand indicates that he is anointing the sick man with a soothing elixir which brings him slumber. In the background, the painter has adorned the rock with two doors through which dreams come and go. Through one door, made of ivory, come deceptive visions, through the other, made of common horn, the true and genuine ones.'

As was customary in Greece, the oracle of Amphiaraus predicted less what would *happen* than what ought to be *done*. This is apparent from the following lines by Pindar, in which Amphiaraus admonishes his son Amphilochus (*Fragments*, 30): 'Child, in all the cities you associate with, make your mind like the skin of the sea-beast clinging to a rock. Readily praise that which is of the present, but, if times change, let yourself change with them.'

EVI MELAS

37

Pottery model of a temple from the Heraeum. Before 600 BC. British Museum, London.

The Argive Sanctuary of Hera

'Too weak my mouth to list the many noble things of which the land of Argos has its share . . .'

Pindar, *Nemean Odes,* x, 19

Argolis was already associated with the cult-legend of the goddess Hera in Mycenaean times. The palace of Mycenae was at once an abode of princes and the deity's place of worship. Written sources state that Hera was regarded as the palace goddess, protectress of military chieftains and spouse of the king. In Homer's *Iliad* (4, 51) Mycenae, together with Argos and Sparta, is named as a city which enjoyed her particular favour.

Tiryns, in Mycenaean times the second largest city in Argolis, also played a major role in the history of the Hera cult. According to Pausanias (II, 17, 5), Tiryns was the home of the goddess's earliest cult-statue, a wooden image carved by Pirasus or Argos and brought to Argos after the city's destruction. According to Clement of Alexandria this cult-statue was a 'long column' (*kion makros*) which the priestess of Hera used to adorn with ribbons and tassels.

In Argos itself, 'Hera's abode, worthy of her majesty', written tradition has it that several temples sacred to the goddess existed in historical times. Greatly celebrated was the temple of Hera Akraia, which stood at the foot of the citadel, but the oldest and most famous sanctuary of Hera was the Heraeum, situated five miles from the modern town of Argos on a hill called 'Euboia'.

From Vitruvius (*De architectura*, III, 1) we learn that the first temple of Hera was built by Dorus, legendary progenitor of the Dorians. The tradition relating to the early founding of the Heraeum has been confirmed by archaeological research. Hera's cult-site was unearthed by American archaeologists in the latter half of the nineteenth century.

Remains of Cyclopean walls and numerous small finds all point to the early structural development of the sacred precinct, but its history proper can only be traced from Homeric times onwards, the period when Argos was regarded as Hera's 'favourite' city. Homer, indeed, gives the goddess the epithet 'Argive'.

Homeric 'theology' transforms the 'queen' of Mycenaean times into the queen of heaven. Hera is now accorded pre-eminence among the female deities of Olympus. She is the spouse of Zeus, father of men and gods, and her ultra-sacred status as his wife makes her the true patroness of women and marriage. The many titles bestowed on her (e.g. 'Teleia', 'Ogygia', 'Gamestolos') have marital associations and account for her main function in historical times. They also point to Hera's 'prehistoric' origin and link her with the great mother- and earth-goddess of the matriarchal period.

Modern visitors to the Heraeum will derive scant information from the visible relics of Homeric date. Massive terraced walls constructed of huge blocks of stone, together with a 65-ft section of the stylobate and three of the temple's column bases, still survive on the north side of the sanctuary. Archaeologists have tried, by studying its foundations and consulting written sources, to reconstruct the goddess's 'first' temple: Doric, with a cella (great hall), and having 6 × 14 slender columns of wood or stone which probably supported a wooden roof. The cult-image was kept in the cella. The founding of the temple took place late in the eighth century BC or early in the seventh. Apart from the numerous small finds made here, these sparse architectural remains provide our chief source of information about the sanctuary's history during the eighth and seventh centuries.

As for the history of the cult, major importance attaches to the small objects that have come to light: rich ceramics, numerous clay or metal idols in animal or human shape, articles of bronze and iron or of precious materials such as ivory imported from the East. Now preserved in the National Museum at Athens, these finds are votive offerings and almost all originated in local Argive workshops. What makes them so important is that figurative representations can be identified, interpreted or confirmed with the aid of written sources relating to the local cult of Hera. Geometric-style vase-paintings of fish, horses, female processions or

choral dances, for instance, can be construed as 'attributes' or 'scenes' associated with the legend of Hera or her local cult. The horse may be expressive of her function as protectress of animals and of her relationship with Poseidon (who was worshipped in horse-breeding regions). Pausanias states that Poseidon and Hera disputed over the land of Argos, and that Phoroneus, Cephissus, Asterion and Inachus decided in favour of Hera.

Although the willow branches and plants carried in procession by women are universal in the Geometric and Early Archaic language of art, they remind us that Hera also bore the title Antheia (goddess of flowers), probably an allusion to her role – inherited from the great nature-goddess of Mycenaean times – as patroness of growing things.

The choral dances or female processions recall the ritual dances which were traditionally performed in the sanctuary in honour of the patroness of maidens and married women. One is tempted to link these female figures on early vases of Argive origin with references by later writers to the celebrated festival of Hera in which all Argive women took part. This major festival, known as the 'Heraea', was held annually and

Cleobis and Biton, sons of the priestess of Hera. Delphi Museum.

occupied a special place among the many festivals sacred to the goddess. The Heraea are construed as a memorial to the mythical marriage between Hera and Zeus. A large train of armed men and gorgeously attired, garlanded women set off from the city of Argos to the sanctuary of the city-goddess, led by the priestess of Hera in a wagon drawn by cows. The office of priestess must have been an important public position because each year took its name from the holder, and lists of such names have contributed greatly to our knowledge of the city's history.

Herodotus recounts that on one occasion the draught-cows failed to arrive from the fields in time. The priestess's two sons, Cleobis and Biton, harnessed themselves to the cart and, watched admiringly by those who were taking part in the procession, hauled their mother all the way to the sanctuary. The priestess craved a boon from the goddess in return for her sons' prodigious feat. While sleeping off their exertions in the sanctuary, they died a peaceful, painless death – the greatest 'boon' which any mortal could have received from an immortal. An inscription on two Archaic monumental statues preserved in Delphi Museum, an early sixth-century votive gift from the Argive people, identifies them as Cleobis and Biton and corroborates the anecdote recorded by Herodotus.

The cows traditionally said to draw the priestess's wagon have an undoubted connection with the early legends about Hera. Cow-idols found in the palace at Mycenae have given rise to the theory that there was a goddess in bovine shape. Numerous votive cows in clay, together with a magnificent statuette in bronze and several in ivory, also came to light in the Argive sanctuary. These finds, most of them in Geometric and Archaic style, readily suggest an association with the hecatombs, votive offerings of a 'hundred cattle'; these were the celebrated sacrifices made during the Heraea. This festival spanned three days, like a wedding. Gymnastic and musical contests were held in honour of Hera 'of the ox-eyes'. The prize awarded to the winners was a shield (doubtless from the metalwork-shops for which Argos was famed) or a myrtle-wreath. The games were also known as the Aspis (*aspis en Argei* = shield in Argos) or Bronze Agon (*chalkeios agon*). Their somewhat martial flavour may well have been an echo of Hera's early function as protectress of citadels. The choral dances performed inside the sanctuary to the strains of flute-music, like the cult-ceremonies traditionally said to have been performed beside the bridal couch (*gamike kline*), suggest a connection with the mythical sacred marriage (*hieros gamos*). Also associated with these rites is Hera's bath in the spring of Canachus, near Nauplion. According to tradition, the goddess bathed in its waters every year to regain her virginity.

The sanctuary's foundations and imposing terraces are all that survive to convey its splendour in classical times. The 'first' Late Geometric temple was destroyed by fire in 423 BC. Pausanias relates that it 'burned down while the priestess Chryseis lay asleep, the torches having set the garlands ablaze'. The new, monumental temple was constructed between 420 and 400 BC. According to Pausanias, its architect was Eupolemus of Argos, who is otherwise unknown to us. Only the foundations of the stylobate (57 × 121 ft) can still be seen. Many fragments of its rich sculptures in Parian marble have survived and are preserved in the National Museum at Athens. These sculptures adorned the pediments and metopes of the temple and were mythical in theme. The east pediment displayed the birth of Zeus, the east metopes a Gigantomachy (battle of the Giants); the west pediment illustrated the destruction of Troy, and the west metopes the Trojan battle with the Amazons. The sculptors' names are unknown; all that can be said with certainty is that various artists worked on the temple's sculptural decoration. Features reminiscent of the great Argive sculptor Polyclitus are unmistakeable, as is Attic influence. Evidence that some of the sculptors had trained in Athens can be found in the fluid, linear rhythm and modelled folds, which recall the masterpieces of the Parthenon, or in the diaphanous drapery, which is reminiscent of the balustrade of the temple of Nike. Indigenous style is apparent in the heavy Argive treatment of form. No

Part of the sima with ornament of tendrils and palmettes, and a fragment from the Heraeum showing two cuckoos, sacred to the goddess. National Museum, Athens.

◄ The remains of the new temple, seen from the terrace of the old Heraeum.

less delightful are the floral acroteria, the frieze of tendrils and palmettes on the sima, and Hera's sacred bird, the cuckoo. The sculptures on the temple of Hera are of major importance to the history of Greek sculpture at the time of the Peloponnesian War because they provide the finest example of the Attic *koine* (artistic language), an amalgamation of various stylistic elements: Ionic, Doric and – probably – Insular Ionic.

The remains of the stoa, at the south-west corner of the site.

The temple of Hera housed the goddess's celebrated cult-statue by Polyclitus. Descriptions by ancient writers and coins of the Imperial era give us some idea of this vanished masterpiece. 'The statue of Hera is seated on a throne,' relates Pausanias (ii, 17, 4), 'a work by Polyclitus in gold and ivory, of goodly size. She wears a chaplet on which are portrayed the Charites [Graces] and Horae [goddesses of the seasons]. One hand holds a pomegranate, the other a sceptre with a cuckoo perched thereon.' A chryselephantine statue of Hebe by Naucydes, Polyclitus' younger brother, is said to have stood beside the goddess's cult-image.

The rich decoration of this classical cult-statue consisted of attributes recalling the goddess's earlier functions. The seated pose and the sceptre in her hand marked her out as queen of heaven and consort of the king of the gods. The pomegranate was an allusion to her role as a bringer of fertility and exemplified her link with the great earth-goddess of primeval times. The cuckoo was a relic of the mythical marriage between Hera and the supreme celestial deity. Its presence is further confirmation of the myth according to which Zeus, eager to seduce the virgin Hera, transformed himself into a cuckoo which she was hunting. The fruit of their union was no doubt symbolized by the statue of Hebe and its proximity to the cult-statue of Hera.

The entire precincts of the Heraeum underwent monumental reshaping after the middle of the fifth century BC: a new temple of Hera was erected in the centre of the great terrace, and strong retaining walls were built to compensate for differences in level. The site was enclosed by colonnades and, in the east, by a four-bayed hall similar to the Eleusinian Telesterion (cf. p. 80). These buildings served as an arena of religious and political activity; no longer used merely for the reception of votive gifts, they provided shelter for participants in the festival of Hera.

The gymnasium west of the sanctuary, site of the contests mentioned by Pausanias, did not originate until Roman times. The temple precinct was bounded by Roman thermae situated north of the gymnasium. Written sources enable us to trace the great festival of Hera into the third century AD. Today, only foundations and archaeological finds testify to its erstwhile splendour.

LILA MARANGOU

The ruins of the temple of Artemis.

Brauron : the Sanctuary of Artemis

With sacred image and your sister, go ;
and, having come to Athens' pile divine,
a place you'll find in outmost Attica,
there where it marches with Carystus' reefs,
a sanctuary called Halae by my folk.

Thus, in his play *Iphigenia in Tauris*, does Euripides describe the position of Halae, now Loutsa, at the southern entrance to the Gulf of Euboea. It was to Halae that the goddess Athena bade Orestes take the wooden statue of Artemis which he had stolen from the Tauri, there to erect a temple to Artemis and introduce her worship. His sister Iphigenia, priestess of Artemis in the land of the Tauri, was to accompany him. Her story is well known. The Greek fleet, ready to sail for Troy, was waiting vainly for a favourable wind. Agamemnon, the Greek commander, vowed to propitiate the gods by sacrificing his daughter Iphigenia. When the sacrifice was made Artemis saved Iphigenia (so that she might serve her among the Tauri) by placing a hind on the altar in her place. Iphigenia was compelled to assist at human sacrifices in the land of the Tauri, was rediscovered there by Orestes and escaped with him to Greece. She became priestess of Artemis at Brauron, where she was privileged to serve the goddess in the Greek manner; following her death there, her tomb became a place of worship.

The sanctuary of Brauron, only 2½ miles from that of Halae and associated with it, fared better than the sanctuary of Halae itself. There was a Brauronium, or shrine of Artemis Brauronia, on the Acropolis at Athens (cf. p. 25). This enhanced the importance of Brauron and diminished that of neighbouring Halae. Ancient writers refer frequently to Brauron and only rarely to Halae, though the name 'Brauron' was

49

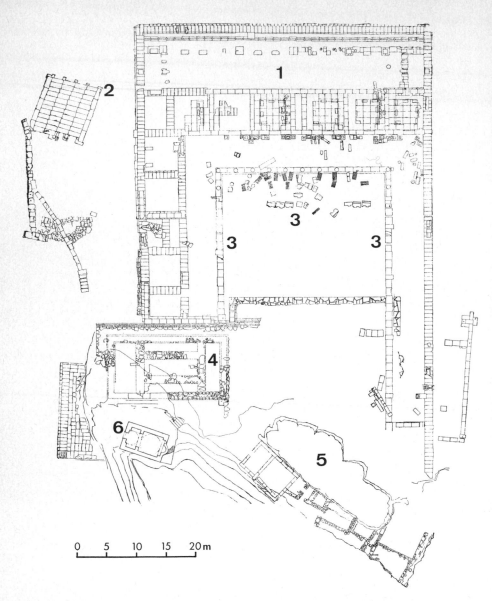

Plan of the sanctuary: 1, display area for garments presented to Artemis; 2, bridge; 3, stoa; 4, temple; 5, tomb of Iphigenia; 6, church of St George (16th century).

sometimes applied to both sanctuaries and, on occasion, to a whole coastal district of eastern Attica.

Only the foundations of the temple at Halae survive, and the sacred precinct is now covered with modern buildings. Brauron remained untouched. Excavation began two decades ago, and the core of the sanctuary has now been laid bare. To judge by the quantity and condition of the finds made hitherto, many more discoveries are likely.

The site adjoins the north-west spur of the lofty hill on which pre-historic Brauron stood, near the harbour of the same name, which was a favourite port of embarkation for the Aegean islands and Asia Minor.

On the hillside, situated higher than the other buildings, archaeologists discovered a Doric temple of Artemis dating from the sixth century or early decades of the fifth century B C. The altar stood near it on a small rocky plateau to the south-west, now occupied by the little church of St George. The level ground below yielded remains of a large rectangular portico or stoa whose three Doric colonnades separated it from the temple precinct to the north. Columns and other structural members have been re-erected. A low bridge to the east is somewhat older than the stoa, which dates from the fifth century. On the south-east slope is a cave – the empty tomb or cenotaph of Iphigenia.

Excavations made to date indicate that the sanctuary of Artemis had no connection with prehistoric Brauron. The decision to erect a sanctuary appropriate to the cult of Artemis may have been prompted by the location of the site, with a major harbour near by (Artemis was the patroness of harbours – hence the epithets 'Limenitis' and 'Limenosco-pos'). Like all sanctuaries of Artemis, Brauron boasted abundant springs and dense woods which well befitted the goddess of the chase. Artemis was also the patroness of rivers, and the Erasinus – now an underground stream – used in ancient times to flow through the Vale of Brauron.

Whatever the origin of the Artemis cult in Attica, its character at Brauron was certainly rustic. Philological sources and archaeological finds leave no doubt that Brauron – a unique example – remained a major centre of rustic divine worship. Artemis Brauronia was patroness of crops – hence the sickles and viticultural implements dedicated to her – and of bulls, horses and goats. Inscriptions show that there were mangers in the sanctuary and that worshippers presented Artemis with

Relief discovered in the sanctuary, showing Artemis with goat and kids, 4th century BC. National Museum, Athens.

bridles and trappings. A finely worked relief of the fourth century BC found in the sanctuary shows Artemis feeding a goat and three kids. Both at Brauron and at Halae, Artemis bore the title Tauropolos (tender of bulls), a name associated with foreign cults as well, e.g. by Euripides in *Iphigenia in Tauris*. Etymologically, however, the word is definitely Greek and has parallels such as Hippopolos, or tender of horses.

Archaeological research has also shed light on the goddess's relationship with handicrafts. Finds included *epinetra*, or earthenware knee-guards worn by women while spinning, and *agnythes*, earthenware weights attached to the end of threads in a vertical loom to provide the correct tension. Like other goddesses, Artemis carried the gold distaff from Homeric times onwards. A fourth-century relief from Brauron shows her spinning and wearing the conventional knee-guard. Women used to dedicate *epinetra* to the goddess, together with hanks of raw wool.

At Brauron, being a goddess of fertility, Artemis was patroness of women in childbirth and of young children. As a lover of the chase, she was also invested with masculine qualities: vases and clay reliefs found here show her armed with bow and arrow and surrounded by dogs, stags or bears. This would likewise account for references in inscriptions to her association with physical exercises in the gymnasium and palaestra (a smaller building), though these buildings have yet to be discovered. The goddess's association with dancing would also have been connected with physical skills. Prayers for fertility were often accompanied by dances, and vases show young girls dancing round the altar. Singing contests were also known at Brauron, and are said to have provided the tyrant Pisistratus or his successors the Pisistratids with a model for the rhapsodes who recited epics at the Panathenaea. Evidence found so far suggests that Artemis Brauronia retained only the positive elements in her ambivalent character. The negative aspects were transferred to Iphigenia, who was jointly worshipped at the sanctuary of Artemis. Euripides says that the finely woven *peploi* of women who had died in childbirth were dedicated to Iphigenia, whereas a commentator referring to the poet Callimachus remarks that Artemis used to be presented with the garments of women who had enjoyed an easy birth.

The earliest finds made at the tomb of Iphigenia date from the seventh century BC, the period at which Iphigenia first makes her appearance in poetry. Hesiod says that Artemis made Iphigenia immortal by transforming her into Hecate. The Homeric hymn to Artemis (early sixth century) lauds the goddess's qualities: she is the venerable virgin and courageous huntress who roves through the mountains with her golden arrow, up to the wind-girt crags. The rocks tremble, the forests roar and the earth shakes. Sated with the chase, Artemis betakes herself to Delphi, to the sumptuous abode of her beloved brother Apollo. Hanging her bow and arrow on the wall, she dons her finery and, to the accompaniment of Apollo's singing, performs the dances of the Muses and Graces. These extol Leto, mother of Apollo and Artemis, for having borne two such children. Leto, Apollo and Artemis became popular figures at Brauron, as the reliefs there show.

But where had Artemis come from when she went to Delphi? In accordance with the realistic character of Archaic poetry, her point of departure must have been a major place of worship actually situated not far from Delphi. This suggests Brauron. Another pointer is supplied by the rhapsodes mentioned above and their contests at Brauron. The short Homeric hymns to the gods were not, in fact, independent poems but introductions to songs by rhapsodes.

The goddess's official festival, the Brauronia, was held every five years and a minor festival annually. The procession of the Great Brauronia appears to have started from the Brauronium on the Acropolis. It lost none of its lively popular appeal, even in classical times. Aristophanes' *Peace* (421 BC) mentions that countryfolk used to follow the procession to an accompaniment of drums, singing joyfully. Once the procession reached Brauron, however, the festivities took a mystic turn. A goat was sacrificed, and young girls known as 'little bears' (the bear was one of the goddess's sacred beasts) processed round the altar wearing crocus-yellow robes and carrying baskets filled with votive gifts.

These 'little bears' are undoubtedly the same as those whom we see depicted on Greek vases dancing round the altar of Artemis. They probably carried the consecrated chitons (garments of wool or linen worn next to the skin) presented to the goddess by grateful mothers after childbirth. Entreating equal good fortune for themselves, they pointed to their robes and hailed Artemis as 'Chitoneia'. Similar consecrated articles of dress were also used in the sacred chase, a symbolic rite based on the goddess's mythical exploits as a huntress. In the course of the Brauronia, the goddess's wooden cult-image was ritually clad in its most gorgeous robe. Her attire was supplemented with pieces of precious jewellery, whole lists of which occur in extant inscriptions.

Dedicatory reliefs from the sanctuary (latter half of the fourth century BC) give a vivid picture of the Brauronian cult of Artemis. Groups of devotees – men, women and children – can be seen approaching the altar to sacrifice a bull. During her 'manifestation' (*epiphaneia*) Artemis is shown standing or seated at the altar with a hind beside her, bow in one hand and a torch or bowl in the other. Devotees, attired in all their finery, stand before the apparition with ecstatic faces. The standing goddess, clad in a *peplos* and holding a bowl, may well be modelled on the celebrated cult-statue which Praxiteles produced for the Brauronium on the Acropolis in the fourth century BC.

Many typical finds in marble, mainly statues of boys and girls, date from the same century. Most of them hold a bird or some other creature

Votive reliefs showing Leto, Artemis and Apollo, and (below) a family making sacrifice to Artemis, 4th century BC. National Museum, Athens.

Statue of a 'little bear', one of the girls dedicated to the goddess Artemis who took part in the Brauronia, 4th century BC. National Museum, Athens.

in one hand and a few hold a fruit in the other – gifts for the goddess. Many more male than female figures have been found, so it is probable that more boys, the guarantee of a family's security and survival, were consecrated to the sanctuary for a given period. Most of the children thus consecrated had undoubtedly lost their mothers at birth and were in need of expiation and divine favour. The children were probably housed in the largest building of all, the colonnaded stoa. Along the north side, which is better preserved than the rest, were rooms with marble tables and holes sunk into the floor to take bed-legs. Beyond the rooms to the north was a passage with a propylon (formal entrance) on each side and a roof supported by columns. Wooden posts once fitted into notches in the floor beneath, so the hall may be assumed to have been a sort of show-room for visitors. The wooden clothes-stands probably held dead women's garments which had been dedicated to Iphigenia.

The great stoa was called the 'Parthenon' (from *parthenos*, meaning virgin, as Artemis and Iphigenia were known). We may take it that the entire structural complex, together with its annexes, was consecrated to the first, mythical, priestess of Artemis. An inscription of the third century BC records the erection of buildings in the sacred precinct by the Athenians in honour of Artemis 'for the preservation of their demos'. The fact that they wrote *demos* (people) and not *polis* (city-state) indicates that the dangers they feared were internal. Artemis, who was also the guardian of communal life within the State, bestowed good fortune on the just and meted out penalties to the unjust.

Because Athens had not always tended the sanctuary at Brauron, however, it is fair to surmise that the Athenians' building activity there had been prompted by an acute threat of some kind. The construction of the stoa may have been occasioned by the sacrilegious mutilation of the Hermae in Athens and by the burlesquing of the Eleusinian Mysteries in 415 BC. Archaeological finds seem to match these dates. Such incidents could only have been provoked by enemies of the demos and assailed its most vulnerable spot: traditional worship of the gods, which the 'modernists' – who were fundamentally reactionary – regarded as primitive and superstitious and, in demonstration of their own 'progressive' ideas, transformed into an object of ridicule. Initial public concern, to which many contemporary sources refer, soon yielded to unbridled hysteria.

Reliable evidence suggests that the tragedy *Iphigenia in Tauris* was first staged – or 'taught', as the Greeks used to say – in 414 BC. This was no coincidence. The plot is closely linked with the Artemis cult which had its home in the two temples on the east coast of Attica. Artemis Tauropolos emerges in the tragedy as a figure purged of the superstitious and barbaric features cited by 'enemies of the people' in their endeavour to shake the faith of the masses. Euripides' Iphigenia is the most human figure in all Greek tragedy. Goethe's *Iphigenia*, which was based on it, became the eighteenth-century incarnation of humanity.

The decline of the ancient religion also spelt the end of the Brauronian sanctuary, and the precinct fell into decay. In the sixth century AD an early Christian church was erected for local peasants a little further to the west. In the sixteenth century the church of St George was built on the small plateau which in antiquity had been levelled for the altar of Artemis.

JOHN KONDIS

General view showing the approach road and the temple of Apollo.

Delphi : the Sanctuary of Apollo

An ancient tradition told how Zeus dispatched two eagles from either end of the cosmos to determine the centre of the earth. The birds met at Delphi, which was henceforward known as the *omphalos* or 'navel' of the world. This tradition was reinforced by the votive gifts in navel-form which were sent to the Delphic oracle for many centuries; one of these is an impressive eagle-adorned *omphalos* of the fifth century BC. A later *omphalos* can be seen in the museum at Delphi (see p. 68).

Geographical reality accords with legend to the extent that Delphi stands at the junction of routes running from eastern Greece to the Gulf of Corinth and from south-west to north. As the oracle's reputation and influence grew, so Delphi became the spiritual centre of the Greek world, a place visited by individuals in quest of advice and by delegations from Greek cities and every country in the known world.

The Homeric hymn describes the ascent to Delphi. Climbing the slopes overlooking the plain of Crisa, one skirts snow capped Mount Parnassus and its precipitous flanks, until, round a bend, a gorge opens before the eye. The view of the cliffs of the Phaedriades ('shining ones') makes an overwhelming impact. 'It is as though a mighty earthquake had cloven the place in two. Earthquakes are a commonplace in Delphi. The south side of the gorge is flanked by the rocky Desphina, known in antiquity as Cirphis, a mountain of medium height and nondescript appearance. However, its very neutralness and sombre colouring help in drawing attention to the opposite side which belongs to Apollo. The Pleistos flows along at the foot of the mountain and joins the sea at Kirra. Immediately above the river, the stony, uneven soil of Delphi rises with varying degrees of steepness to the Phaedriades, tinged with shimmering silver by ancient olive-trees. One is constantly aware of the cloven abyss. There beside the Castalian spring, where the Phaedriades have their roots, is the putative chasm of chasms: the two rock walls are separated by a sharp cleft – now known as "Bear Gorge" – which extends far down into the plain of Pleistos' (Christos Karousos).

The easternmost of the Phaedriades soars 2,300 ft into the blue sky. When founding his sanctuary, Apollo chose its western neighbour, less wild and known as 'rose-red' because the dawn steeps it in a rosy light. According to the Homeric hymn, he once abducted some Cretan merchants bound for Pylos and, in the shape of a dolphin, guided their ship to Crisa. From there he brought the Cretans to his sanctuary, which was still known as 'Pytho' and only later acquired the name 'Delphi'. The Cretans became his priests, and Apollo promised them a perpetual abundance of herds.

The town of Delphi remained a modest place; its inhabitants – a figure of roughly one thousand is quoted in the fourth century AD – would never have aroused the envy and greed of others had it not been for the oracle's limitless wealth. From the seventh century BC onwards, Delphi formed part of the Amphictyonic League, an association of neighbouring cities and tribes. The members convened at Delphi in autumn and in spring at the sanctuary of Demeter at Anthela, near Thermopylae.

In the course of 250 years, four holy wars were waged to safeguard Delphi's independence and free access to its oracle and sacred precincts. The neighbouring towns of Crisa and Amphissa received exemplary punishment from the League members.

All major Greek cities sought to intervene in the affairs of Delphi so as to resolve disputes and thereby boost their own influence. The holy wars all occurred in the oracle's first phase, i.e. between the eighth and fourth centuries, when its impact on the Greek ethos was strongest and extended to the kings of Lydia, Egypt and Phrygia. When the temple of Apollo was destroyed by fire in 548 BC, its reconstruction was financed not only by Greek cities but also by King Croesus of Lydia and the Pharaoh, Amasis, both of whom sent vast sums of money.

In the critical period preceding the Persian invasion (fifth century BC), the Delphic oracle failed: the Greeks' decision to resist the Persians to the last received no divine confirmation. Apollo's priestess, the Pythia, clearly overawed by the enemy's superiority, did not venture to give them oracular encouragement (Herodotus, VII, 140). On the contrary, the Athenian envoys were treated to a dire warning, but to the Athenians, with Themistocles guiding the destinies of their city-state, the moment was an auspicious one. They made a vital contribution to the famous Greek victory at Salamis, and after the Persians had been successfully repulsed, the Athenians and other Greeks forgave the Pythia and sent large numbers of votive gifts to Delphi.

Legendary riches accumulated there over the centuries. After the death of Alexander the Great in 323 BC barbarian invaders were magically attracted by the Delphic temple treasures, and the place was repeatedly saved as though by some miracle of divine intervention. Tempests, snowstorms and rock-falls impressed enemy forces so mightily that they fled, one example being the Galatians in 279 BC. The latter event was commemorated by the Soteria, held in honour of Zeus the Saviour (Zeus Soter) and Apollo. The oracle lost some of its prestige from Hellenistic times onwards. Although it was still consulted by common folk and the rulers of every known land, Apollo had lost his erstwhile power and initiative. Speaking through the Pythia, the god merely confirmed the wishes of those in power, those who paraded votive offerings of supreme magnificence.

The great despoliation of Delphi, which continued for centuries, began when Greece was occupied by the Romans. The Roman general, Sulla, purloined numerous votive gifts in 86 BC, and three years later Delphi fell prey to a Thracian tribe (on which occasion the sacred flame in the temple of Apollo was allegedly extinguished for the first time). Nero robbed the sanctuary of another five hundred statues in AD 67. Pilgrims still journeyed to Delphi and isolated attempts were made, e.g. by the philhellene Emperor Hadrian, to restore its ancient splendour – indeed, Pausanias mentions having seen valuable treasures there in the second century AD – but the triumphal progress of Christianity set the seal on the fate of the once-mighty oracular shrine. The extent to which devotees themselves recognized this is apparent from an oracular pronouncement which Oribasius, the envoy of the Emperor Julian, is said to have received at Delphi:

> Tell your master this: destroyed is the place blessed with skill; Phoebus has neither abode nor prophetic laurel; the spring no longer serves him, and silent is the murmuring water.

The Tholos, a marble rotunda of *c.* 390 BC, adjacent to the temple of Athena Pronaea on the Marmaria terrace.

◄ The temple of Apollo, with the steep face of the Phaedriades beyond.

It was during Delphi's prime, or between the eighth and fifth centuries BC, that the ancients evolved their conception of the god who played a leading role in all Greek affairs by resolving conflicts and schooling men in morality, tolerance and prudence.

According to one tradition, Apollo vanquished the earth-cult that preceded him without resorting to force. Gaea, the earth-goddess and 'protomantissa' (first prophetess) was succeeded on the oracular throne by her daughter Themis; Themis voluntarily ceded her position to Phoebe, the Titaness, and the latter presented the place to Apollo as a birthday gift. In gratitude, Apollo assumed the name Phoebus – or so Aeschylus tells us in the *Eumenides*. Poseidon was also worshipped at Delphi conjointly with Gaea, not as a sea-god but – as in other cities in the Gulf of Corinth – as the god of springs, rivers and earthquakes. The Muses, too, resided at Delphi even earlier than Apollo and were allotted their own shrine as custodians of the 'mantic spring'. Later, they became companions of the new god. Impressed by Delphi's grandiose scenery and the rocky gorge, the ancient Greeks doubtless surmised that this was where Gaea, mother of all living creatures, mistress of the underworld and a goddess who knew all there was to know about man and his destiny, had chosen to reveal some of her secrets. The ancient gods, notably Gaea, retained their sanctuaries at Delphi, though only in a marginal capacity.

According to other mythical sources, some of them conflicting, Apollo did not come to power without a struggle: he first slew Python, the 'reddish-scintillating serpent in the shade of the luxuriant bay tree, the earth-born, huge-bodied monster, guardian of Gaea's oracle' (Euripides, *Iphigenia in Tauris*, 1245). Apollo 'purified' himself in the Vale of Tempe and went into self-imposed exile at the court of Admetus, King of Thessaly, where he worked as a slave to atone for the blood he had shed. He thus provided the earliest indication that bloodshed does not necessarily call for revenge, and that murder can be expiated by other means. Apollo proclaimed this more humane way of purging blood-guilt, or *katharsis* (purification), through the medium of his oracle. Aeschylus makes the avenging Furies (or Eumenides) lament: 'Ah, ye newer gods, ye tread the old laws down. They are wrested from our grasp.'

Phoebus, the radiant Apollo of Delphi, aspired to moral purity for himself and mankind. 'He is versed in healing, banishes the evil spectre, and every house becomes pure by his power' (Aeschylus, *Eumenides*, 62–3). In the Homeric hymn to Delian Apollo, the new-born god declares: 'Mine be the lyre and curved bow, them will I love; and I proclaim Zeus' unerring counsel to mankind.'

Apollo, the 'beloved son of Zeus', knew his father's will. His prophetic utterances reached men through the mouth of the Pythia; through the priestess, he counselled them on their actions and conduct, and taught them to meet their destiny by acting 'moderately', within the proper limits 'which always exist'. The Delphic dictum 'Know thyself', which was carved on the temple of Apollo, originally referred to human impotence vis-à-vis the gods. Its later implication was more encouraging: self-knowledge enables a man to use and fully exploit his capacities.

Delphi influenced the Greeks during their second great migration between the eighth and sixth centuries BC. The oracle directed Greek colonists from the Black Sea to Africa, from Asia to the Pillars of Heracles (Gibraltar). Delphi also played an important role in political decisions, the founding of new States, municipal constitutions and the conduct of war. Legislation initiated *c.* 600 BC in Sparta by the reformer Lycurgus was approved by Delphi. It was the Pythia, too, who selected from a list of one hundred names of traditional Attic heroes the ten whom Cleisthenes (founder of Athenian democracy) nominated as progenitors of the ten Athenian *phylae* (tribes).

Apollo demanded tolerance and practised it himself by permitting the cult of Dionysus, a god utterly opposed to him in character, to share his abode. Between December and February Apollo abandoned Delphi for the mythical land of the pious Hyperboreans, a place of never-ending day and eternal spring. In winter, therefore, the Pythia's oracular voice fell silent. No paeans, or ceremonial hymns to Apollo, were heard; instead, dithyrambs (choruses) rang out and festivals were held in honour of Dionysus. When springtime came, Apollo returned to his Delphic sanctuary in a car drawn by swans – a scene often depicted on vases.

The major Delphic festival, or Pythian Games, was held to commemorate Apollo's victory over Python. In very early times, musical contests took place every eighth year in commemoration of Apollo's eight-year period of atonement in the Vale of Tempe. Pausanias (x, 7, 3) relates that Hesiod and Homer were excluded from the contest, the former because he had not learnt to accompany himself on the cithara, the latter because of his blindness.

From 582 BC onwards, after the end of the first holy war, these contests were reorganized by members of the Amphictyonic League. Athletic events and horse-races now took place in the hippodrome. The Pythian Games, which lasted six to eight days, were henceforth celebrated every four years in August–September, after the Olympic Games. Tragedies and comedies subsequently formed part of the festival, in which victorious contestants were awarded laurel-wreaths.

Three months before the start of the Pythian Games, envoys from Delphi proclaimed a 'sacred armistice' throughout the land. Their lengthy route took them to many cities which they duly summoned to take part in the games. The envoys, known as *theoroi*, set off in festive procession and were everywhere received with jubilation. An added reason for this advance announcement of the Pythian Games was that Greece had no common calendar.

Detail of the frieze of the Siphnian Treasury, *c.* 525 BC.

We know that the games opened with animal sacrifices. Until 342 BC, Apollo's battle with Python was symbolically re-enacted after sunset on the first day. On the *halos* (threshing-floor) beside the ancient shrine of Gaea, a representation of the serpent's nest was erected. Apollo's role was played by a boy whose parents had to be living. Members of the Labyathian *phratria* (clan), flaming torches in hand, assisted the boy up the steps; from above, he aimed his bow at Python's nest while the torch-bearers set it ablaze. This done, everyone hurried off without looking back and underwent ritual purification.

The second day of the Pythian Games was marked by a splendid procession of priests and official envoys. Competitors marched to the altar of Apollo, where the public sacrifice of a hecatomb (a hundred beasts) took place. Musical contests were the principal feature, however, especially a hymn to Apollo. The fifth day was devoted to athletic contests and the sixth to equestrian events and chariot-races. Pindar paints a vivid picture of the ceremonial chariot procession over twelve

Columns of the temple of Apollo, completed in 330 BC.

laps of the hippodrome. Legends speak of three 'mythical' temples of Apollo, the first of laurel, the second of beeswax and feathers, and the third of bronze. There were three historical temples, too, but of stone; the ruins visible in the sacred precincts today are those of the third stone temple, completed in 330 BC on the exact site of its two historical antecedents. The first had been built c. 650 BC and destroyed by fire a century later; the second was completed c. 510 BC. Fragments of its Attic frieze sculptures are displayed in Delphi Museum.

The temple's vestibule was adorned with the maxims of the Seven Sages: 'Know thyself' and 'Nothing in excess', also the still unexplained letter 'E' and a bronze head of Homer. At the entrance to the laterally divided cella (great hall) stood the iron throne from which Pindar had reputedly intoned hymns to Apollo. It was generally believed that the poet's shade still lingered there. Every evening the priests sent a messenger who called out: 'Pindar is bidden to sup with the god!' and invited the spirit to enter the temple, where a table was laid for two.

An *omphalos* representing the navel of the world (see p. 59), and (right) the Naxian Sphinx which stood on an Ionic column over 33-ft high, close by the 'rock of the Sibyl'; both pieces are now in the museum at Delphi.

In the forepart of the cella stood the hearth of the goddess Hestia, home of the eternal flame which burned in the name of all Greece. The rear portion or adyton (inner sanctum) was on two levels. It consisted of a ground floor which housed the gold cult-statue of Apollo, and a lower-ground floor divided by a thin wall into the *oikos* (where those in quest of counsel assembled) and the *antron* (to which only the Pythia had access). The *antron* contained the 'prophetic' fissure which emitted the intoxicating vapour inhaled by the Pythia as she sat on her tripod and prophesied what Phoebus imparted to her. As she did so, she touched the *omphalos* or navel-stone which the ancients regarded as the tomb of Python or Dionysus. Beside her, water trickled from the spring of Cassotis.

Archaeologists who excavated the temple found a stone slab furnished with recesses for the tripod and *omphalos*, also a channel. Plutarch, who held priestly office at Delphi for years, leaves no doubt in his description

68

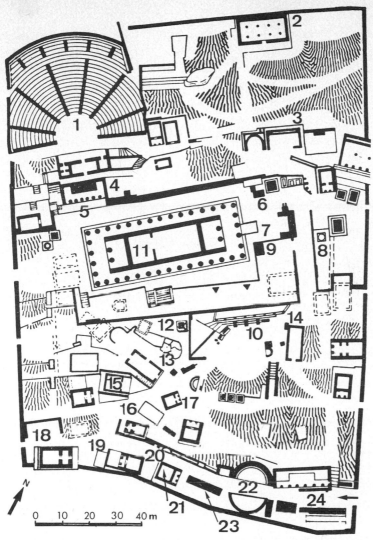

Plan of the sanctuary: 1, theatre; 2, Lesche of the Cnidians; 3, group by Daochus of Thessaly; 4, find-spot of the bronze Charioteer of Delphi; 5, Craterus memorial; 6, columns of Prousias II of Bithynia; 7, altar of Apollo; 8, tripod from the booty of the battle of Plataea (479 BC); 9, column of Aemilius Paullus; 10, stoa of the Athenians; 11, temple of Apollo; 12, Naxian column; 13, 'rock of the Sibyl'; 14, treasury of Corinth; 15, Athenian treasury; 16, treasury of Syracuse; 17, treasury of the Cnidians; 18, treasury of Thebes; 19, treasury of Megara; 20, Siphnian treasury; 21, treasury of Sicyon; 22, votive offering of Argos; 23, treasury of Tarentum; 24, votive offering of Athens for the victory at Marathon. Drawing by W. Konnertz.

that the fissure was within the temple and approached by a flight of steps, but the geology of the place rules out the idea of vapours arising from the ground.

The *theopropoi* or oracle-seekers sat in the *oikos*, next door to the Pythia's *antron*, and put their questions in a loud voice. The inarticulate cries of the Pythia, who was in a state of ecstasy, were interpreted by priests. Women were strictly forbidden to enter the adyton.

There was only a single Pythia at first, but she was later joined by one or two others. Originally held by young girls, the soothsayer's office later went to selected fifty-year-old women of attested virginity. They had their own quarters in the sacred precinct and dressed like young girls, presumably in memory of the first, youthful, Pythia. Pythia and *theopropoi* had to purify themselves in the 'silver' Castalian spring before consulting the oracle. They also sprinkled the temple with its waters.

The *theopropoi* had to pay the shrine a fixed sacrificial fee and slaughter an animal, usually a goat. The beast was first sprinkled with water. If its entire body began to tremble, the god was deemed to be present and the oracle might be consulted. Plutarch informs us that this condition had to be strictly fulfilled or the Pythia would have been in mortal danger. The ceremony was performed by the priests of Apollo, in other words, the three 'prophets' and the five *hosioi*, who were priests of Dionysus. Right of consultation (*promanteia*) was vested in the inhabitants of Delphi and granted to those who had rendered service to their town.

In ancient times the priests' oracular pronouncements were couched in the form of a couplet consisting of one hexameter and one pentameter. Prose took over from the third century onwards. The responses were frequently so ambiguous that oracle-seekers misconstrued their meaning: in the sixth century BC, for example, Croesus of Lydia misunderstood the prediction that he would destroy a great empire if he crossed the Halys. Immediately thinking of hostile Persia, Croesus launched an attack on King Cyrus and delivered Lydia – his own large empire – up to destruction.

Half-way through the first century BC, Cicero asked the Delphic oracle how he could win greater fame. The god responded that he must let his actions be ruled by his character and not by the opinion of others. Questions, however, ranged from the naïve ('Shall I marry?' – 'Shall we

The Sacred Way leading to the restored Treasury of the Athenians.

till our fields?' – 'Is it worth travelling to . . . ?' – 'Will the harvest be good?' – 'Is my wife faithful?') to highly complex problems of settling disputes between cities and countries or squabbles between classes and families.

Scanning the sky as he ascends the steep Sacred Way which winds upwards from terrace to terrace through the temple precinct, the visitor will see descendants of the 'birds of Zeus', proud eagles which nest in the Phaedriades and soar in wide arcs above the ruins.

Of the numerous buildings and statues consecrated to the god, most survive only in the form of inscribed bases and plinths – mute testimony to pan-Hellenic victories, to fierce fratricidal wars between Greek cities and, last but not least, to many a ruler's personal ambition. One glowing exception to the general run of monuments, which tended to commemorate Greek disunity, is the votive offering, decorated by Phidias, which the Athenians erected beside the first section of the Sacred Way

71

Detail of the retaining wall of the temple of Apollo which is covered with inscriptions incised in the stones.

after defeating the Persians at Marathon in 490 B C. Much criticism and disapproval has been aroused since the days of antiquity by all the stone memorials to victories by the Greeks over Greeks. Perhaps such critics have overlooked the childish pride which inspired victors to transmit their city's triumphs to posterity, like a prize won in some sporting contest. Battle and contest – the Greek word *agon* can, after all, mean either.

The second section of the Sacred Way begins with the now-restored Athenian Treasury, an architectural masterpiece in the form of a small Archaic temple. Its walls, which are covered with inscriptions, bear two hymns to Apollo dating from the second century B C.

Delphi's oldest cult-relics lie close at hand. Reputed to have prophesied here on a crude block of stone is the priestess of earth-mother Gaea, the first Sibyl who came from Asia Minor, possibly from Erythrae. Here, too, was the mantic spring guarded by Python, further east the rock from which Leto, mother of Apollo, exhorted her son to do battle with Python, and finally the circular threshing-floor (*halos*).

The treasury dedicated by the Athenians in 478 B C, immediately after the Persian Wars, is a finely articulated building with seven Ionic marble columns, and attracts particular attention. The inscription on the stylobate of grey Parnassus stone ('The Athenians dedicated this treasury, together with the arms and prows which they seized from the enemy') revives memories of victorious sea-battles against the Persian king, Xerxes. Behind the building extends the 275-ft retaining wall of the temple of Apollo, constructed of large polygonal blocks of stone bearing inscriptions of the second and first centuries B C – itself an archive in stone.

Beside the last section of the Sacred Way, before it reaches the temple of Apollo, there stood in ancient times two impressive monuments: a golden tripod on a tall bronze Serpent Column presented by thirty-one Greek cities which had helped to defeat the Persians at Plataea in 479 B C, and, opposite it, an altar dedicated to Apollo by the island of Chios.

Above the temple of Apollo, at the northern end of the sacred precinct, stood the Lesche (communal hall) of the Cnidians, which once contained a mural painting by Polygnotus (*c.* 460 B C). To the west of this one can still see the theatre (second century B C) which seated 5,000, and, considerably higher up the mountainside, the stadium.

Heraclitus once said: 'The lord to whom the oracle at Delphi belongs says naught and conceals naught; he gives signs.' Even if Delphi did err in its oracular pronouncements, its credibility remained unimpaired until the end of classical antiquity. The god's signs had simply been misconstrued by mortal men.

ATHINA KALOGEROPOULOU

73

General view of the sanctuary and the acropolis at Eleusis, seen from the north.

Eleusis : the Origins of the Sanctuary

Strict secrecy surrounded all that occurred in the Eleusinian sanctuary and the ritual of the Mysteries; this accounts for the paucity of information – much of which conflicts – that has come down to us. The death penalty awaited anyone who divulged anything connected with the cult of Demeter and its secret rites. Aeschylus, who made veiled references to the Mysteries in some of his tragedies, narrowly escaped indictment for blasphemy on that account. Alcibiades and his friends were condemned to death *in absentia* because they had burlesqued the Mysteries. Even Pausanias took care not to describe the Eleusinian sanctuary.

Our lack of information is compensated to some extent by ruins dating from every period in the sanctuary's centuries-long history. Their good state of preservation is attributable to the great awe in which the Eleusinians held their oldest shrine, also to the steepness of the slope on the east side which made it necessary to build stout retaining walls for every extension to the existing buildings – which were thereby also preserved. As a result, Eleusis is the only archaeological site in Greece where surviving ruins enable one not only to reconstruct a picture of what used to be but to trace the sanctuary's structural history from its founding in Mycenaean times to its eventual destruction in the fifth century AD.

The Society of Dilettanti began to dig at Eleusis in 1812, and a further attempt to excavate the sanctuary was undertaken by François Lenormant in 1862. The scope of these operations remained severely limited, however, because the site was then occupied by the small town of Eleusis. It was not until 1882 that systematic excavation was undertaken by the Archaeological Society of Athens, which had previously bought and demolished all the houses and removed the township to its present position. Numerous vases and sculptures connected with the cult were found, also inscriptions which supply important information about the topography and identification of various buildings.

We know that ever since the Mysteries became a pan-Hellenic cult they were celebrated twice a year: the so-called 'Lesser Mysteries' in the month of Anthesterion (March) and the 'Great Mysteries' in Boedromion (September).

During the Lesser Mysteries participants were 'purified' and prepared for their final initiation in the sanctuary of Demeter at Agrae, beside the Ilissus in Athens, and hence they were also known as the Mysteries of Agrae. The Great Mysteries began on the fourteenth day of Boedromion and ended on the twenty-second. On the opening day, priests from the Eleusinian sanctuary led by the hierophant (priest) and *daduchos* (torch-bearer) brought the 'sacred objects' (*hiera*) from the inner sanctum of the Eleusinian sanctuary's Telesterion (hall of initiation), where they were kept, to Athens. Here they were taken into the other Athenian sanctuary of Demeter, the Eleusinium below the Acropolis. Next day the hierophant and ceryx, senior dignitaries of the Eleusinian sanctuary, went to the Poikile or Painted Stoa in the Athenian Agora and solemnly inaugurated the public festivities, in which all Greeks, slaves included, were allowed to participate; only murderers and those who could not speak Greek were barred.

Sacrifice and rites of purification were performed between the sixteenth and eighteenth days of Boedromion. On the nineteenth came the splendid climax of the festival, the return to Eleusis. The hierophant removed the sacred objects from the Eleusinium. Preceded by a statue of Iacchos, who was worshipped in association with Demeter, the festive train set off along the Sacred Way very early in the forenoon. It reached Eleusis, 13½ miles distant, after sunset. During the last two nights, the twenty-first and twenty-second of the month, the great festival of the Mysteries was held in the Telesterion. Although we now have a clear idea of the Eleusinian sanctuary and are acquainted with the 'public' rites connected with the Mysteries, our knowledge of the 'secret' rites and their content is little more than speculation (cf. Samothrace, p. 193). Secrecy was strictly observed.

In prehistoric times, Eleusis was an independent kingdom which controlled the fertile lowlands, the Thriasian Plain of antiquity. Bounded

The Callichoron spring which was regarded as sacred by the ancient inhabitants of Eleusis.

by lofty mountains, the plain abutted on the sea in the south. Near the coast stood two low hills, one in the west and the other east of it. The western hill was steeper and higher and has since been quarried away.

Eleusis was founded *c.* 2000 BC on the eastern hill. During the Mycenaean period it developed into a powerful city and, by virtue of its favourable situation, became chief rival to Athens. At this time the hill-top site was fortified with a ring-wall. At its north-east extremity, above the cave of Pluto, stood the palace of Celeus, king of Eleusis, commanding a broad expanse of plain. Below the palace, where the sanctuary's main entrance lay in historical times, was the Callichoron spring which supplied the city with drinking-water; so important was this spring that the Eleusinians regarded it as sacred and their young girls honoured it with dances.

The Homeric hymn to Demeter, a very ancient poem probably composed *c.* 600 BC and recited in the course of the Great Mysteries, has

preserved certain traditions about the origin and development of the
Eleusinian cult of Demeter:

One day, when Demeter's only daughter Persephone was
frolicking with her friends on the Banks of the Eleusinian river,
at a spot named Erineos, the ground opened. Pluto, god of the
underworld, emerged in his chariot and carried Persephone off
into the depths of the earth. The goddess Demeter, unable to see
her child and consumed with fear, hurriedly descended from
Olympus. Vainly she combed the world for traces of Persephone.
Exhausted, she sat down beside the spring Callichoron, where
the daughters of King Celeus encountered her and conducted her
to the palace. Out of gratitude for so hospitable a welcome, she
became governess to the king's little son, Demophon, whom she
proposed to make immortal. Queen Metanira, surprised by the
preternatural development of her little son, secretly watched one

Relief from Eleusis,
showing Demeter giving
the first ears of corn to
Triptolemus. National
Museum, Athens.

night as Demeter held Demophon above the fire. The queen
cried out and wept with fear. Angrily, the goddess cut short her
work, revealed who she was, and bade the people of Eleusis erect
a temple and altar to her somewhat below the city beside the spring
Callichoron, near the wall on the hill [*Prouchon Kolonos*]. The
goddess shut herself up in this temple, and forbade the earth to
bear fruit. A great famine ensued, but, when the people died in
droves, Zeus suffered Persephone to return from the underworld
and henceforth dwell for two-thirds of the year with her mother
on Olympus. Demeter's rage abated. She bestowed new fruit-
fulness on the earth and, before leaving Eleusis, called the archons

Reconstruction of the Mycenaean megaron discovered at Eleusis.

[rulers] together, taught them how she should be worshipped, and revealed to them the mysteries, which would help those who strictly observed them to a better existence on earth and a life of bliss in the underworld.

Other traditions give different versions of how the Eleusinian cult of Demeter originated, but the Homeric hymn reflects the most widespread and best-known variant. Its precise description of the temple site accords perfectly with the topography of the sanctuary at Eleusis. The *Prouchon Kolonos,* or 'forward-jutting hill', does actually form a natural terrace below the city and above the spring of Callichoron. This is the spot where later generations built the Telesterion, the unique temple in which the goddess Demeter was worshipped and the Mysteries were celebrated. Precisely here, beneath its pavement, the archaeologist K. Kourouniotis discovered in 1931 the remains of a Mycenaean megaron whose important bearing on the origin of the Eleusinian sanctuary has been rightly

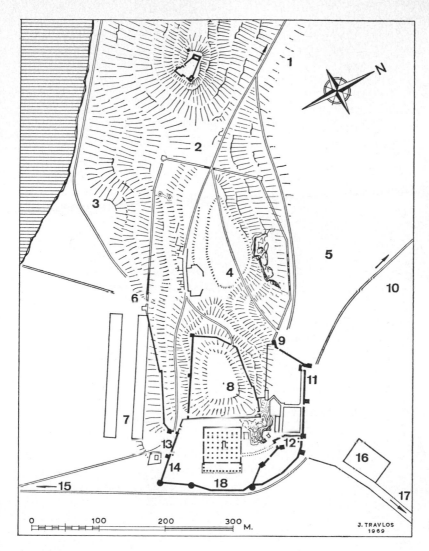

Plan of Eleusis: 1, road to Megara; 2, Megara gate; 3, theatre; 4, town; 5, hippodrome;
6, gate to stadium; 7, stadium; 8, acropolis; 9, west gate; 10, road to Thebes; 11, city gate;
12, Smaller Propylaea; 13, south gate; 14, Periclean wall; 15, road to harbour; 16, Pompeium;
17, road to Athens; 18, sanctuary.

stressed. Its very presence beneath the Telesterion leaves no doubt that this was the earliest sanctuary of all, the first site of the Demeter cult.

Was it a temple erected at the goddess's behest, as the Homeric hymn says, or are we dealing with an even older building into which the cult of Demeter moved and in which it took root? The ruins enable us to reconstruct a megaron, or ordinary residence of the time. This closely resembles the much-scaled-down clay model of a house from the Heraeum at Argos, which has been interpreted and reconstructed by the archaeologist G. Oikonomos.

Enclosed by thick walls, the megaron probably accommodated an archon from one of the two ancient clans of Eleusis, the Eumolpidae and Ceryces. That it was a residence is additionally betokened by three rooms of later date built on to the north side. It would be more than strange if they had been erected immediately adjoining a temple. I believe that the megaron found beneath the Telesterion was the residence of the Eumolpidae, one of the two families which had been granted control over the sanctuary and the Mysteries.

The residence of the other family, the Ceryces, which developed into an independent sanctuary as time went by, must be identical with the 'House of the Ceryces' mentioned in an inscription dating from 329-328 BC concerned with 'statements of accounts of the epistatae of Eleusis'. This building stood on the north side of the hill beside the Plutonium, with whose cult it was – in my view – closely connected.

The Eumolpidae, on the other hand, were directly associated with the cult and temple of Demeter. The family had always occupied a leading priestly role. The name of their ancestor is linked in the Homeric hymn with the genesis of the cult of Demeter and – according to other philological sources – with the ancient history of the city of Eleusis. Eumolpus was a son of Poseidon and led the Eleusinians in battle against Erechtheus, the mythical king of Athens. This tradition is reflected in the struggle between Poseidon and Athena for mastery of Athens.

Eumolpus' Thracian origin permits us to infer the cult's place of origin. It was initially confined to the residence itself, the Mycenaean megaron which has been dated to the latter half of the fifteenth century BC. Thus the cult was at first private and did not assume a local significance until later. The megaron was now devoted exclusively to the

The temple of Demeter, 6th century BC.

cult, and the three rooms on the north side were constructed as living-quarters at the beginning of the thirteenth century BC.

From then on, the sanctuary of Demeter enjoyed an uninterrupted existence. Its core, the Mycenaean megaron, was replaced during the construction of the first Telesterion by a small temple, the adyton or inner sanctum, but was still known as the megaron out of respect for tradition. Its site remained constant, although the Telesterion underwent numerous alterations between the seventh century BC and the second century AD.

The 'sacred objects' were carefully preserved in the adyton, which no one apart from the hierophant was permitted to enter. The fact that this supreme priestly honour remained the prerogative of the Eumolpidae would seem to be yet another proof of the family's hereditary rights, and reinforces my theory that the cult originated in their residence.

The history of the sanctuary during the Geometric period and up to the building of the first Telesterion *c.* 600 BC has yet to be fully

Plaster model of the sanctuary as it would have appeared in the 2nd century A D, based on plans by John Travlos. Eleusis Museum.

investigated. The earliest ruin of that period is a curved wall near the megaron, on the east side. The foundations of this wall repose on the southern stretch of the destroyed Mycenaean perimeter wall. Most authorities date it to the eighth century B C, but it could well have been constructed at the end of the ninth. It is often assumed to have been the foundation of a building, but the careful dressing of the east face alone permits us to conclude that it was a retaining wall designed to reinforce the earth slope in the large courtyard in front of the megaron.

The official introduction of Demeter's cult coincides with the Eleusinian Mysteries' assumption of pan-Hellenic character in the middle of the eighth century B C; at that time a strong new retaining wall was built east of the curved wall. (Only the corners on either side of the Pisistratean Telesterion have survived.)

Although there are no traces of the temple which originated at the same time as the courtyard, it is certain that the megaron and adjacent living-quarters were already demolished and their ruins buried beneath

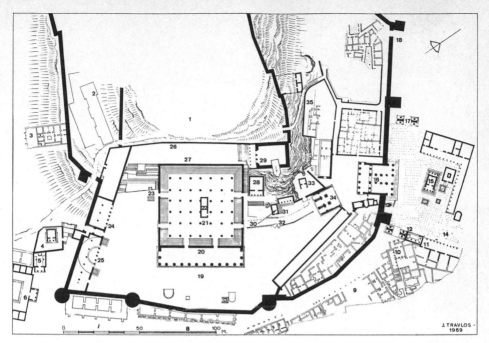

Plan of the sanctuary of Demeter in the 2nd century A D: 1, acropolis; 2, museum; 3, Roman houses; 4, sacred houses; 5, Mithraeum; 6, market place; 7, artificial pond; 8, springs; 9, visitors' accommodation; 10, baths; 11, stoa; 12, spring; 13, Callichoron spring; 14, Sacred Way; 15, temple of Artemis; 16, great Propylaea; 17, ceremonial gates; 18, city gate; 19, sacred court; 20, Portico of Philo; 21, Telesterion; 22, Anaktoron; 23, altar; 24, stoa; 25, Bouleuterion; 26, Diateichisma; 27, rock terrace; 28, treasury; 29, Roman temple; 30, temple of Hecate; 31, exedra; 32, ceremonial way; 33, Plutonium; 34, Smaller Propylaea; 35, house of the Ceryces.

the surface of the courtyard. F. Noack assumes that the yard contained nothing but an altar at which the festival was held. Since the 'sacred objects' would necessarily have required special accommodation, however, I incline to the view that a small temple was constructed on the site of the Mycenaean megaron, possibly of wood or sun-dried brick.

The time at which retaining walls and courtyard were constructed coincides with the fifth Olympic Games (760 B C). The new buildings must have been connected with an official renovation programme, the undoubted intention being to appease and placate the goddess so that she would check the great famine which was then raging in Greece. The Delphic Oracle had bidden the Athenians sacrifice to Demeter in the

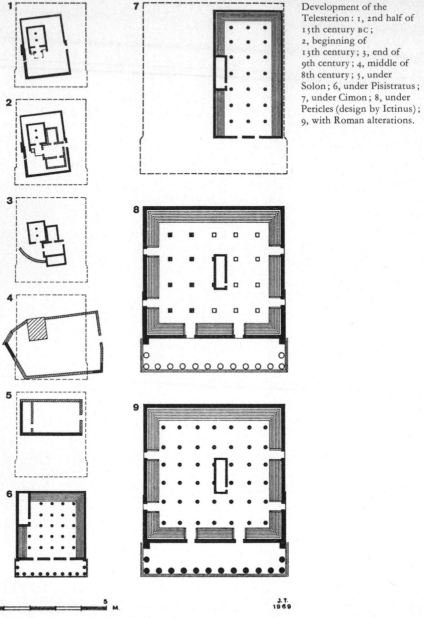

Development of the Telesterion: 1, 2nd half of 15th century BC; 2, beginning of 13th century; 3, end of 9th century; 4, middle of 8th century; 5, under Solon; 6, under Pisistratus; 7, under Cimon; 8, under Pericles (design by Ictinus); 9, with Roman alterations.

0   5 M.

J. T. 1969

name of all Greeks. A festival known as the Proerosia was duly introduced before the spring sowing.

From that time onwards, the private houses of Eleusis fell into decay and their place was taken by the ever-expanding sanctuary of Demeter. One section of the new wall of this period still stands north-east of the Telesterion, but its continuation is buried beneath the sixth-century wall. The sanctuary's great reputation and the building of the first monumental Telesterion, whose surviving ruins afford us a clear idea of its original appearance, date from the time of Solon, c. 600 BC, at which time Eleusis was finally united with the city-state of Athens and the Homeric hymn is assumed to have been composed. The cult of Demeter and Persephone gained ground, and the Eleusinian Mysteries, together with the Great Panathenaea, became the Athenian city-state's greatest festival.

The Eleusinian sanctuary of Demeter was enclosed by a strong new wall which encompassed Eleusis itself and was designed to safeguard a city of such importance to the Athenians and their security. The new fortifications were also meant to cover their lines of communication with the Peloponnese, Thebes and northern Greece.

The sanctuary continued to expand, and attained its greatest compass in the middle of the fourth century BC. Meanwhile, the city spread westwards to the furthest hills. Although the sacred precinct formed a continuation of the city and enjoyed the protection of a common perimeter wall, it was separated from Eleusis proper by another wall whose purpose was to preserve the secret of the Mysteries. However, the sacred precinct was itself divided by a wall: on one side lay the courtyard with the Telesterion overlooking it, on the other the priests' quarters, administrative buildings and annexes. These distinctly separate parts were none the less linked by a propylon (gate) dedicated to Demeter and Persephone.

Eleusis ceased to have an independent history after Solon's time. It became one of the large Attic demes (communities) and shared the destinies of the metropolis. Solon, Pisistratus, Cimon, Pericles and Lycurgus all cultivated the sanctuary's reputation and added new buildings. The Roman emperors, who respected the Mysteries, endowed Eleusis with its greatest lustre in the second century AD; this it retained until the sanctuary was destroyed in the fifth century.

J. Travlos

Relief of the 4th century BC, showing Asclepius, now in the National Museum, Athens.

Epidaurus : the Sanctuary of Asclepius

Situated on the east coast of the Peloponnese, the district of Argolis extends from the high mountains of the hinterland to the Aegean Sea. At its heart, bordered by low hills, lies the undulating plain of Epidaurus.

From Mycenaean times – i.e. about the sixteenth century BC – Epidaurus was the domain of Maleatas, a god of healing later amalgamated with Apollo, who henceforth bore his predecessor's name as a surname. Apollo Maleatas was worshipped on Mount Kynortion, which rises on the edge of the sacred precinct of Epidaurus. Excavations carried out in 1948 brought to light numerous relics of sacrifices made here during the seventh century BC. Ruins of a fourth-century temple of Apollo Maleatas and buildings dating from subsequent centuries show that the cult on Kynortion survived without a break until Roman times.

How and when Asclepius, son of Apollo, came to Epidaurus and ousted his father is not known. The late Ioannis Papadimitriou was of the opinion that Apollo reached Epidaurus during the seventh century BC, and Asclepius during the sixth. Homer refers to Asclepius as mortal, a Thessalian king versed in the art of healing. The ancients enlisted legends to account for his promotion to demigod and god. These legends agree that Asclepius was the son of Apollo and a mortal woman; they conflict in the matter of his birthplace. The inhabitants of Tricca (modern Trikkala), in Thessaly, invoking the fact that Asclepius' first sanctuary was founded there, claimed him as a scion of their native city.

The story of Asclepius' birth is recounted in *Ehoiai,* an epic poem attributed to Hesiod: 'In ancient times there dwelt in Thessaly a king's daughter named Coronis. One day, as she was bathing in the sea, Apollo became enamoured of her and coupled with her. Shortly thereafter her father compelled her to wed Ischys, a man of royal lineage whom he had chosen for her. The raven, bird of Apollo, espied the wedding preparations and conveyed the news to his master. Enraged, the god first punished the bird which had brought him the evil tidings and turned its feathers, which has hitherto been white, black; then he dispatched his sister Artemis, who slew Coronis with her arrows . . .'

Pindar (522–448 BC) gives this version: 'Coronis, who was with child by Apollo, deceived him, unbeknown to her father, with Ischys son of Elatus. Coronis was sentenced to be burned alive. At the very moment when her body was consumed by flames, Apollo intervened and saved the child.'

The people of Epidaurus transferred the story of Asclepius' birth to their own sanctuary in order to enhance its reputation. At Delphi too the priestess of Apollo, the Pythia, mentioned in an oracle that 'Coronis gave birth in rocky Epidaurus'. Isyllus (third century BC) wrote in his hymn to Asclepius that Coronis was the daughter of a native, Phlegyas, and brought Asclepius into the world at Epidaurus. Finally, Pausanias (in the second century AD) related that Phlegyas, followed by his daughter Coronis, arrived in the Peloponnese unaware that she was expecting a child by Apollo. When the child was born, Phlegyas exposed it on Mount Tithion. The new-born babe was suckled by a goat and guarded by a dog . . .

All ancient writers concur that Apollo entrusted the Centaur Chiron with the rearing of his son in Thessaly. Chiron, the sage mentor, had brought up such mythical and legendary heroes as Achilles, Jason, Castor and Polydeuces. Asclepius was initiated by him into the art of medicine. He learnt to distinguish between poisonous and curative herbs (which still grow on Mount Pelion), perform miracles, mitigate suffering and cure diseases. In later times, allegories of health, recovery, relief and physical well-being were transformed into members of the god Asclepius' family. His two sons, Machaon and Podalirius, were physicians. When Menelaus, one of the Greek generals in the Trojan War, was wounded, Machaon was summoned to heal him. Hygieia, the goddess of health, was regarded as a daughter of Asclepius.

According to one theory, Asclepius dates from pre-Hellenic times, when he was worshipped as an earth-spirit. His symbol (or attribute?) was the serpent, a creature which knew the secrets of the underworld and

The famous theatre on the west slope of Mount Kynortion, built by Polyclitus the Younger at the end of the 4th century BC.

was credited with prophetic powers because it could glide silently from fissures in the earth and vanish into them once more. It was thought that the dead, too, could appear in serpent-form. Others construed the fact that snakes shed their skin every spring as a symbol of resurrection.

Pausanias asserts that the snakes kept at Epidaurus were pale brown, of medium size, and harmless. They were held to be sacred and occasionally assumed the functions of Asclepius himself. Hence the serpent coiled round the Aesculapian staff (Asclepius = Latin, Aesculapius), the badge of the medical profession today. In myth, Asclepius dies. (It will be remembered that the god had a mortal mother.) Asclepius' death is a token that, although of divine origin, medical science cannot (or may not) transgress the laws of nature. When Asclepius ventured to raise the

Statues of the goddess Hygieia, *c.* 370 BC, and of Asclepius, found at Epidaurus. National Museum, Athens.

dead, Hades, lord of the kingdom of the dead, complained to his brother Zeus, ruler of Olympus. The latter struck Asclepius down with his thunderbolt and killed him.

As faith in the gods of Olympus waned over the centuries and superstition gained the upper hand, so the power of Asclepius grew. People sought relief from physical and mental suffering at his sanctuary, which acquired pan-Hellenic importance. The date of its foundation is unknown, but future excavation may shed light on the subject. The oldest votive inscriptions to Apollo and Asclepius were found beside the altar in the temple and date from the sixth century BC, and references to the noted sanctuary can be found in fifth-century authors. The cult spread from Epidaurus, and several more sanctuaries of Asclepius were built.

All the ruins now visible at Epidaurus date from the fourth century BC. The sanctuary belonged to the ancient city of Epidaurus, which lay below it at the sea's edge and is now submerged. A hill north of the great temple precincts has been identified with Mount Tithion, another in the east with Mount Kynortion. Two broad roads led to the sanctuary, one through the mountains from Epidaurus and the other through the plain from Argos; they converged just short of the place.

Pilgrims visiting Epidaurus in its prime (fourth–first centuries BC) passed through the propylaea, the fourth-century ceremonial gateway with Ionic columns, and trod the Sacred Way which led to the festival site and temple. They passed a stone slab inscribed with the welcoming words: 'When you enter the god's house, which is scented with fragrant herbs, you must be pure, and your mind is pure when you draw near in reverence.' Water flowed from a small spring near by. No walls enclosed the sacred precinct, but its boundaries were marked out. An ancient law forbade women to give birth there, and sick people on the verge of death had to leave the sanctuary.

The temple of Asclepius had been built by the architect Theodotus in the fourth century BC. The building had eleven Doric columns along the sides and six at either end. The floor was paved with black and white marble slabs. A large wooden door with ivory ornamentation and gold nails was the work of Thrasymedes of Paros, who had also produced the cult-statue of Asclepius, an over-life-size, majestic figure in gold and ivory, its kindly countenance framed by a beard. Asclepius was shown seated on a throne, one hand holding his staff and the other touching the head of the sacred serpent; the sacred dog, his other attribute, lay at his feet. The statue, which has disappeared, was seen by Pausanias, whose description matches representations to be seen on many coins, and two votive effigies in Epidaurus Museum. The temple was painted in bright colours, and its splendour and magnificence were enhanced by the sculptures on the pediments, acroteria and sima. The Epidaurus Museum displays a part-reconstruction of the temple. The original remains have found their way to the National Museum at Athens.

A paved road ran past the temple to the sacred spring, whose water was used for purification by the faithful. They visited the temple and made sacrifice, then entrusted themselves to the priests for treatment. The chief priest of Asclepius was appointed to a one-year term of office by the State, and it was his duty to maintain strict observance of ritual, aided by numerous assistants with specially defined powers.

Stories of the miracles wrought at Epidaurus spread throughout the known world. Pilgrims – sick people whom physicians had failed to cure – flocked to the place: the road to the sanctuary was lined with the sightless and crippled, wounded men with spear-points lodged in their bodies, barren women, consumptives and epileptics. Having made sacrifice and cleansed themselves, patients submitted to religious exercises and tests so as to approach the god in a state of due preparedness. The priests used their knowledge of psychology to reinforce the powers of auto-suggestion.

Were the rites performed in the fourth-century circular marble building called 'tholos' by Pausanias and 'thymele' in an inscription? The Tholos, a circular building the ruins of which can be seen north-west of the temple, was the show-piece of Epidaurus, resplendent in its architecture and sculptural decoration. An outer colonnade of twenty-six Doric columns enclosed the cella, with an inner circle of fourteen Corinthian columns. Beneath the central pavement were three circular passages – probably of the sixth century BC – which recall the 'Labyrinth'. We do not know what rites were performed there, or whether this was the abode of Asclepius' sacred serpents. The building was commonly regarded as his tomb.

Fragmentary inscriptions refer to a festival at which specially trained singers (*paeanistae*) sang hymns and paeans in honour of the god. Sophocles wrote a hymn for this festival after Asclepius had commissioned him to do so in a dream. Another hymn, this time by Isyllus, carved in stone can be seen in Epidaurus Museum. Inscriptions expressly state that sacrifice was made to Apollo *and* Asclepius. The cult of Apollo survived, therefore, but Asclepius was credited with any miracles that occurred.

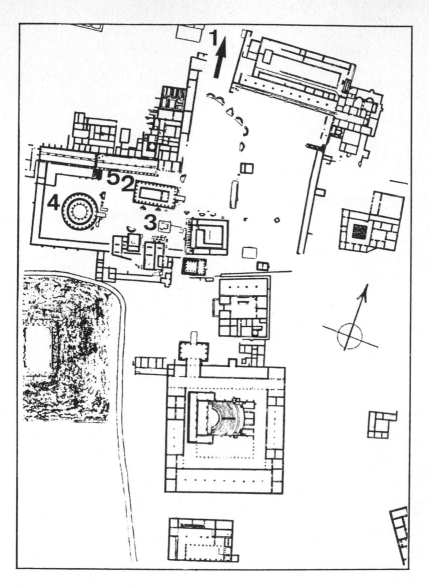

Plan of the sanctuary of Asclepius: 1, propylaea; 2, temple; 3, altar; 4, tholos; 5, abaton.

Although oxen were sacrificed on the altar, cockerels were more frequently used, and the sacrifice of a cockerel could in certain cases avert misfortune and assist women in childbirth. Even today the slaughter of a cockerel on the foundation-stone of a house is said to ward off calamity and misfortune. The meat of sacrificial victims had to be consumed inside the sanctuary. Those without means were permitted to make offerings such as fruit and cakes, and pilgrims could give money.

North of the temple lie the ruins of a 250-ft dormitory with a double Ionic colonnade, a fourth-century building to which another storey was added in the west a century later. This was the abaton or sacrosanct place where patients practised incubation, sleep being an important factor in their treatment. The stelae inscribed with names of patients, their ailments and cures, provide our most graphic information about the miracles wrought by Asclepius. During the excavations of 1882, two intact stelae and fragments of a third were found in the abaton. These announcements of successful cures were probably recorded in conjunction with the building of the abaton in the fourth century BC, to the honour and glory of the sanctuary. Most of the inscriptions, which describe some sixty cures, are naïvely devout in character. All the texts begin by invoking the gods Apollo and Asclepius, also 'kindly providence', but Asclepius alone figures in dreams. Examples of these inscriptions are:

A little dumb child entered the sanctuary to ask the god to give it a voice. After all sacrifices and rites had been performed, a priest turned to the father and asked: 'Do you promise to pay the cost of the cure within a twelvemonth.' 'I promise,' the child replied in a loud voice. Utterly astonished, the father asked his child to repeat what it had said. The child obeyed. It was cured.

Hermodicus of Kampsacon, a cripple, slept in the abaton. The god healed him and bade him, as soon as he left the abaton, to carry a very heavy stone into the sanctuary. Hermodicus fetched the stone, which still lies outside the abaton.

A woman from Messina, Nicoboule by name, ardently desired a child. She slept in the abaton and had the following dream: the god stood before her with a snake in his hand. The snake glided to Nicoboule and slept with her. . . the woman bore twin sons.

Pilgrims had to meet the cost of treatment; the amount, strangely enough, was said to be communicated to patients in their sleep. When the god forgot, his priests presented the bill, which was large for the rich and modest for the poor. The god accepted anything, valuable or trifling: models of healed limbs, vessels of bronze and clay, beds and tables, votive inscriptions recording case histories (the priests being interested in publicity), statues, paintings, even altars and entire buildings such as the temple library.

None of these case histories makes mention of the priests' activities or of medicinal therapy on the god's part. We learn, for example, that the god recommended a cripple – among other pilgrims – to stay in Epidaurus for four months. The patient remained in the sanctuary, which offered him a mild climate, rest, hot and cold baths, and pure drinking-water, until he was cured: 'Eratocles of Troizene was afflicted with a suppurating wound which the physicians proposed to cauterize. The god advised against this and instead prescribed incubation at Epidaurus. When the term stipulated by the god was at an end, the suppurating wound had cleansed itself and Eratocles was cured.' (There was a rumour to the effect that Hippocrates, the founder of medical science, born in Cos *c.* 460 BC, had destroyed the stelae in the sanctuary of Asclepius there because he rejected the idea of divine intervention in medicine.)

Aristophanes, whose mordant wit spared none of the gods, poked fun at the sanctuaries of Asclepius and their activities in his comedy *Plutus*. Chremylus and his servant Carion bring the god of wealth, Plutus, to Asclepius. Plutus, being blind in his distribution of worldly goods, is to be taught to see. The satire is witty and realistic, as can be seen from the excerpt below in the translation by B. B. Rogers:

CARION ...Without we took him to the sea and bathed him [Plutus] there.
WIFE O what a happy man, the poor old fellow bathed in the cold sea!
CARION Then to the precincts of the god we went. There on the altar honey-cakes and bakemeats were offered, food for the Hephaestian flame. There laid we Wealth as custom bids; and we each for himself stitched up a pallet near.
WIFE Were there no others waiting to be healed?
CARION Neocleides was, for one; the purblind man who in his thefts outshoots the keenest-eyed. And many others, sick with every form of ailment. Soon the temple servitor put out the lights and

bade us fall asleep, nor stir, nor speak, whatever noise we heard... he [the god] went round, with calm and quiet tread, to every patient, scanning each disease. Then by his side a servant placed a stone pestle and mortar; and a medicine-chest... ... Well, first he set himself to mix a plaster for Neocleides, throwing in three cloves of Tenian garlic; and with these he mingled verjuice and squills; and brayed them up together. Then drenched the mass with Sphettian vinegar, and turning up the eyelids of the man, plastered their inner sides to make the smart more painful, Up he springs with yells and roars in act to flee; then laughed the God and said: Nay, sit thou there, beplastered; I'll restrain thee, thou reckless swearer, from the Assembly now.

WIFE O what a clever, patriotic God!

CARION Then, after this, he sat him down by Wealth, and first he felt the patient's head, and next, taking a linen napkin, clean and white, wiped both his lids, and all around them, dry. Then Panacea, with a scarlet cloth, covered his face and head; then the God clucked, and out there issued from the holy shrine two great enormous serpents.

WIFE O good heavens!

CARION And underneath the scarlet cloth they crept and licked his eyelids, as it seemed to me; and, mistress dear, before you could have drunk of wine three goblets, Wealth arose and saw. O then for joy I clapped my hands together and woke my master, and, hey presto! both the god and serpents vanished in the shrine. And those who lay by Wealth, imagine how they blessed and greeted him, nor closed their eyes the whole night long till daylight did appear. And I could never praise the god enough for both his deeds, enabling Wealth to see and making Neocleides still more blind.

WIFE O Lord and King, what mighty power is thine!

As time went by, more and more sick people sought help, not from Asclepius but from the Asclepiads, who operated independently of the sanctuaries. All physicians called themselves Asclepiads, tracing their name from Asclepius' successors, among them Hippocrates. The relationship between physician and sanctuary remained undisputed, however, and doctors made votive offerings.

For their part, the priests of Asclepius were prompted by concern for their sanctuaries' survival to follow the dictates of experience and adapt their treatment accordingly. Priests now gave 'consultations' prior to incubation and suggested appropriate forms of therapy. After incubation they interpreted dreams from the aspect of medical experience. The change that had come over the sanctuaries of Asclepius is exemplified by a votive inscription of the second century BC dedicated by one Apellas, whose hypochondria had led to digestive disorders:

> As I was travelling to the sanctuary and neared the island of Aegina, the god appeared and bade me not to worry so unduly. When I reached the sanctuary, he bade me further to cover my head in rainy weather, wash myself without the aid of a servant, take exercise in the gymnasterion, eat bread, cheese, celery and cabbage-lettuce, drink lemon-juice and milk, go for walks and not omit to make sacrifice. Finally, he bade me record all this on a stone. I left the sanctuary cured and grateful to the god.

The sanctuaries of Asclepius gradually developed from religious centres into health resorts like the spas of modern times. Visitors converged from all over Greece to attend the festivals and contests. Many of them lodged in the sanctuary's largest building, the 150-roomed hostel. Epidaurus had much to offer contemporary sightseers, including temples of Aphrodite, Artemis, Athena, Themis and Dionysus.

From the fifth century BC onwards, the Great Asclepia became a pan-Hellenic festival. Every four years the faithful walked in procession from the town of Epidaurus to the sanctuary, garlanded with laurel in honour of Apollo, and olive twigs in honour of Asclepius. The festivals included athletic and equestrian games, and, from the fourth century onwards, as we know from Plato's *Ion*, musical and vocal contests. The theatre, world renowned in antiquity and unique in terms of size, acoustics and architectural beauty, was built on the western slope of Mount Kynortion at the end of the fourth century BC by Polyclitus the Younger.

The sanctuary of Asclepius at Epidaurus survived for almost eight hundred years. Asclepius was the only god of ancient Greece to hold his own against the oriental cults. Suffering humanity could not abandon its hope of recovery – the hope which Asclepius bestowed. Christian sources of the fourth century AD speak disparagingly of those who 'still sleep in the abaton'. When Christianity triumphed, the Christians, in their turn, prayed to SS. Cosmas and Damian for aid in the fight against disease.

ANGELIKI CHARITONIDOU

Figures of Zeus (centre), Oenomaus and Pelops, from the east pediment of the temple of Zeus (see p. 112). Olympia Museum.

Olympia

The valley of Olympia is bounded in the east and north by the mountains of Arcadia. In the north, spurs from the mountains of Elis run down to the sanctuary itself, and the conical hill of Kronos, which always formed the heart of the sanctuary. The rest of the sacred precinct (*temenos*) extends on the west of the River Cladeus to the low hills which give way, in the north-west, to the Drouba Mountains.

The valley is watered by two rivers, the Alpheus and Cladeus, the confluence of which is at Olympia where they were venerated. This is one of the rare places where rivers are at once a life-bringing force and truly awesome spirits. The Alpheus unites the waters of more than ten Arcadian and Elean tributaries and flows through an island-studded bed which expands or contracts according to the season. Even today, embankments have failed to tame the turbulent waters of the Alpheus and every spring and winter the peasants await the floods, wondering how much land the river will wrest from them or, possibly, add to their fields. During the Middle Ages the Alpheus carried away a large part of the sanctuary and hippodrome. The Cladeus, seen when dry in summer, conveys no hint of its power; its flood-waters devastated parts of the gymnasium and other buildings at the beginning of modern times. On the other hand, the two rivers do bestow on the area a fertility rare in Greece. Vegetation thrives in the damp soil, and the ground is carpeted with luxuriant greenery and wild plants bearing flowers of every colour.

The impression of constant flux is accentuated still further by the hills, a loose Tertiary formation. It may have been this landscape, with its absence of clearly defined outlines and air of continuous change, which prompted the ancient Greeks, when worshipping the gods and evolving myths, to people the Olympian sanctuary with so large a number of deities, daemons and heroes. Even now, spirits, sorceresses, Nereids and

General view of the site, from the north-west.

Fates are reputed to dance in the moonlight and manifest themselves to local inhabitants or passing travellers, just as they did in the days of Archilochus.

The same two rivers determined the route of the earliest thoroughfares leading through the mountainous Peloponnese to the extreme limits of that peninsula – a convoluted network of roads. The Alpheus used to be navigable as far as Olympia, which had been a religious festival centre since mythical times. A big agricultural festival used to be held there until the outbreak of the Second World War, and its site in the temple precincts is still known as the 'Paneghiristra' (festival site).

On the southern slope of the hill of Kronos lay a village of which remains dating from the second millennium BC have been excavated. Some finds belong to the Mycenaean period but have no connection with

Ruins of the temple of Zeus, with column drum in the foreground.

the cult, which cannot be historically documented prior to the first millennium BC.

There are conflicting versions of the legend relating to the Olympian sanctuary's foundation. These stem from rivalry between the Pisatans and the inhabitants of the valley of Elis, who vied for its control.

The struggle ended early in the sixth century BC with the defeat of the Pisatans, who none the less refused to accept the loss of the district and waged guerrilla warfare against the Eleans for another two centuries. The Pisatans cited mythological and historical evidence in support of their claim – likewise the Eleans.

It was said, for instance, that Kronos and Rhea had been worshipped at Olympia prior to the birth of Zeus. The quinquennial Olympic Games were, according to one account, founded by Heracles, one of the Dactyls from Mount Ida in Crete, to whom the young Zeus was entrusted to save him from being devoured by his father Kronos. It was also said that Zeus defeated his father Kronos at Olympia, whereas Apollo worsted Ares at boxing. Another tradition, first recorded by Pindar, relates that the sanctuary and games were founded by the Heracles known to us as the son of Zeus and Alcmene. He is also said to have established a sacred precinct in the Altis for his ancestor Pelops, in whose honour the Olympic contests were celebrated henceforward.

> But now, reclining on Alpheus' bank,
> he relishes the fair blood-offerings
> and has his much-frequented tomb hard by
> the altar to which men from all lands come...

These lines from Pindar's *Olympian Odes* seem to conjure up a picture reminiscent of a heroic relief: Pelops gazing keenly at the stadium from his barrow and rejoicing in the fame of the Olympic Games, which were held on the 'tracks of Pelops'. There is no doubt that the Olympic Games still, in the fifth century BC, possessed the death-cult associations which had been customary among Greeks from ancient times.

The hero Pelops, erstwhile king of Olympia and grandson of Zeus, came to be worshipped by the local inhabitants more than any other god, just as Zeus, too, received a greater share of veneration than other members of the pantheon. (Pelops even gave his name to the Peloponnese, the 'island of Pelops'.) The Olympian cult of Pelops did, in fact, enjoy undoubted importance, and the place allotted to it within the sanctuary was only a few paces from Zeus' fire-altar, a mound composed of the ash from burnt offerings. Even when the temple of Zeus was built Pelops continued to be worshipped in its vicinity. Sacrifice to Pelops preceded sacrifice to Zeus, though Pausanias relates that no one who had partaken of a ram sacrificed to Pelops could join in the sacred rites in honour of Zeus. At Olympia, Pelops was the earth-spirit *par excellence,* whereas Zeus retained his Olympian (celestial and earthly) character.

Pelops' barrow was probably a Mycenaean grave subsequently ascribed to the hero through an indirect association between local prehistory and later cult. Traces of a grave were found during low-level excavations,

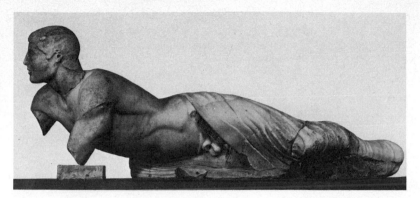

The river-god Cladeus, from the east pediment of the temple of Zeus (see p. 112). Olympia Museum.

but no other remains of any kind. According to Pausanias, all Pelops' remains with the exception of one shoulder lay buried outside the sacred precinct. Pelops' barrow was thus a cenotaph, not a genuine tomb.

Until the first Olympic Games in 776 BC, or during the earliest centuries for which historical evidence exists, Olympia was simply a religious centre serving the farmers and cattle-breeders of the neighbourhood. The number and quality of votive gifts waxed in step with the sanctuary's growing importance. Its oracle, which operated in conjunction with sacrifice on the altar, concerned itself with agricultural problems.

Contests, notably chariot-races linked with the military tactics of the early historical period, seem to have been held at Olympia from ancient times. A tradition of indisputably Elean origin relates that the games were discontinued for some years. The Eleans' royal ancestor, Oxylus, who allegedly guided the Dorians from Aetolia to the Peloponnese, was awarded Elis in return for his services and instituted games at Olympia. These lapsed for a considerable time after his death until Iphitus, one of his descendants, reintroduced them and the sacred armistice which had to be observed for the duration of the Olympic Games to prevent martial interruptions. Oxylus and Iphitus are mythological figures, of course, but no chariot-races took place for some time. We know that they were reinstituted in 680 BC.

Although in 776 BC the games consisted of a simple race run over a distance of 209 yards, the following events had been added by the middle of the seventh century: a race over two lengths of the stadium, a long-distance race, pentathlon, wrestling, chariot-racing and *pancration* (a form of free-style wrestling-cum-boxing), together with equestrian contests. Boys' contests were held in later years.

As Zeus extended his dominion over the whole of Olympia, so the regulations governing the contests developed into a sort of athletic code. Penalties were devised for those who failed to observe the regulations and transgressed this code. Any violation was regarded as an affront to Zeus and a disgrace, not only to the athlete himself but to his native city as well. Awareness of joint responsibility on the part of *polis* and athlete, together with the exceptional honours bestowed on victorious athletes by their cities of origin, were in keeping with the attitude that prevailed during the finest phase of Greek athleticism and the Golden Age of the *polis* and its ideals. Virtue and excellence were no longer the prerogative of those few men who alone counted in politics and warfare. The ideal of virtue had become a goal aspired to by every free citizen, both physically and mentally.

As military tactics changed and the chariot lost ground to the hoplite (heavily armed infantryman), so the cities focused their attention on the individual hoplite and attached greater importance to their citizens' physical prowess. Successful participation in the pan-Hellenic games was a reflection of this concern.

Although equestrian- and chariot-races were not among the most important contests, their reintroduction at Olympia aroused the interest and ambitions of the well-to-do, notably those from Greek colonies in the West, where the concept of democracy enjoyed no particular favour among public men or private citizens. Lured by the urge to see and be seen, tyrants, kings and noblemen of the ancient world travelled to Olympia, where their triumphs were lauded by poets and immortalized in stone by sculptors.

Until the seventh century BC the Altis, or sanctuary, remained Olympia's only place of worship. This was a cult without a temple, a very early form of divine worship and one which survived in some parts of Greece throughout antiquity. In most sanctuaries the altar – the essential focus of worship – was situated in the open, so a special plot of land (*temenos*) had to be set aside.

Olympia's luxuriant vegetation made it particularly suitable for the worship of Zeus because he was the ruler of heaven and earth, of climate and fertility. He was also the god who punished by means of the thunderbolt, as worshippers no doubt recalled when violent storms raged over Olympia. The sound of thunderclaps reverberating from the mountains – Olympia's medieval name was 'Echo' – created the impression that a battle with the Giants was in progress. Zeus, master of gods and men, had the power to bring order and harmony into nature and human existence.

Planes and wild olives grew in profusion in the sanctuary. It was said that Heracles, son of Zeus and Alcmene, had brought cuttings of wild olive to Olympia 'from the shady sources of the Danube', home of the legendary Hyperboreans. One of these olives near the temple of Zeus was known as the 'tree of the fair chaplets' because it supplied the shoots with which athletic victors were crowned.

In very early times the Altis contained numerous altars: apart from the fire-altar of Zeus and the tomb of Pelops, altars to Gaea (Earth), Themis and Hera. These altars were rectangular or circular structures, some of stone and others of clay. Bronze tripods were erected beneath the trees as votive offerings and other votive gifts were suspended from their branches.

The pantheistic character of the sanctuary went back to Heracles, who had founded the altar of the twelve gods. Even in the second century A D, Pausanias speaks of a sacrificial rite duly performed each month, and refers to seventy principal altars. All the gods were represented, some of them in several capacities, also rivers, Nymphs, Charites (Graces), Muses, Fates, the weather, and so forth.

Official sacrifices were made to all the gods every month. They were conducted by the same priest and followed the same ritual, part of it being the decking of altars with olive branches in honour of Zeus. This proves that the various cults were subordinate to Zeus rather than independent. Excavations have shown that the votive gifts found near the altars were essentially similar, a fact which likewise indicates that there was no clear-cut distinction between cults. Olympia's 'pantheon' may be regarded as an assembly of gods subject to the authority of Zeus. Indeed, the cult of Zeus at Olympia betrays certain tendencies towards a monotheism which recurs among poets and philosophers.

The initial phase, during which the Altis had no temple, ended in the mid-seventh century BC when the first temple of Hera was built. Its remains were buried by the more recent, early sixth-century Heraeum whose ruins can now be seen at the foot of the hill of Kronos. This second temple was constructed in the Doric style and enclosed by a colonnade of 6 × 16 wooden columns which were gradually replaced with stone; the cella (great hall) of the temple was of mud bricks; in the background, Pausanias saw the cult-statue of Hera (the limestone head of which was discovered in the course of excavations). Hera was seated on a throne with the bearded and helmeted Zeus standing beside her; this standing pose distinguished Zeus from other statues erected in the sacred precinct, and indicates that he was generally worshipped under the open sky until devotees built him a temple of his own.

Hera's temple (the Heraeum) should probably be attributed to the Pisatan-Argive alliance that was formed when the Pisatans asked King Pheidon of Argos to aid them against the Eleans, for Argos was the Peloponnesian centre of the cult of Hera. The cult of Hippodamia was probably imported from Argos at the same time. The remains of Hippodamia, who was said to have died in Argolis, were conveyed to Olympia on the advice of the Delphic oracle, Delphi being the supreme authority in matters relating to hero-cults. Hippodamia was allotted a sacred precinct in the Altis, and it was to her that people ascribed the institution of girls' foot-races in honour of Hera.

Construction of the Treasuries at the foot of the hill of Kronos began c. 550 BC. Eleven of these small temple-like buildings, in which the city-states' more precious votive gifts were stored, stood side by side facing the Altis, and forming an impressive backcloth for the ceremonial procession to the altar of Zeus.

Until the middle of the sixth century BC, the games were held on the site of the later stadium, though this had yet to assume architectural shape. Contests took place on the level ground below the hill of Kronos, with spectators ranged along and above it. The site was predetermined from the outset by the existence of the altar of Zeus and the grave of Pelops, the hero in whose honour the games were held, who was regarded as watching them in person.

As Olympia waxed in importance, so actual facilities for the games gradually took shape. Excavations have illustrated this development in detail. Olympia enables us to trace the genesis of a specific form of architecture: as with tragedy and the theatre at Athens, so, at Olympia, stadium and athleticism came into being concurrently. Although, even at Olympia, the stadium was never more than a plain unstructured 'ground', in other words, a simple arena bordered by a minimum of stonework, no major elements were added subsequently. It was the product, not of theory, but of practical experience in using the same site for centuries.

The first stadium, dating from the sixth century B C, was replaced by fifth-and fourth-century successors which conformed to changing conditions and ideas. The first two stadia witnessed contests between athletes of the greatest renown. The running-track originally extended far into

Ruins of the temple of Hera, built in the Doric style in the 6th century B C.

the Altis but was re-routed in the third version. Now separated from the Altis by a wall and the so-called 'Porch of Echo', it was enclosed by banks of earth for the convenience of spectators. A judges' platform was also installed. This is the stadium which the modern visitor sees, its air of grandeur obtained by simple means.

The Prytaneum of the Eleans, in which victors feasted at the community's expense, was erected in the north-west corner of the Altis during the fifth century BC. Directly opposite it in the sanctuary's south-east corner stood the shrine of Hestia, goddess of the hearth, and the Bouleuterion (council chamber), two more fifth-century buildings.

The temple of Zeus, built by the Elean architect Libon between 470 and 456 BC, towered in the centre of the sacred precinct, a Doric temple

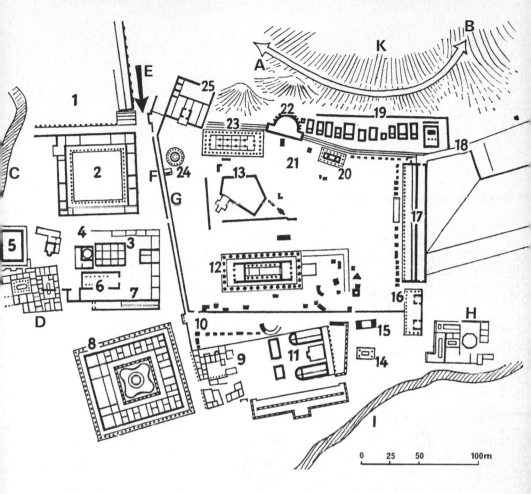

Plan of Olympia: 1, gymnasium; 2, Palaestra; 3, Theogoleon; 4, vapour bath; 5, baths; 6, Byzantine church; 7, workshop of Phidias; 8, Leonideum; 9, hot springs; 10, foundations of Roman portico; 11, Bouleuterion; 12, temple of Zeus; 13, Pelopeum; 14, foundations of a temple of Artemis; 15, triumphal arch; 16, south-east building; 17, Porch of Echo; 18, stadium; 19, foundations of an altar and eleven treasuries; 20, Metroön; 21, traces of dwelling houses; 22, exedra of Herodes Atticus; 23, temple of Hera; 24, Philippeum; 25, Prytaneum. Other references: A, road to Patras; B, road to Tripoli; C, river Cladeus; D, Roman hostel; E, entrance; F, Roman wall of the Altis; G, ancient wall of the Altis; H, Roman buildings; I, river Alpheus; K, hill of Kronos.

◄ Model of the temple of Zeus (centre) and surrounding buildings (see plan above). Olympia Museum.

Detail of the west pediment of the temple of Zeus: Lapiths fighting a Centaur, *c.* 450 BC. Olympia Museum.

Figure of Apollo, from the west pediment of the temple of Zeus, *c.* 450 BC. Olympia ▶ Museum.

approximately 65 ft high and enclosed by a colonnade of 6 × 13 columns; the material principally employed was local limestone.

The metopes of the cella were decorated with the Labours of Heracles. On the east pediment Oenomaus and Pelops stood girded for their mythical contest, a chariot-race for possession of Hippodamia, Oenomaus' own daughter. In the centre: Zeus, thunderbolt in hand, calm but disapproving, as though the impending tragedy were not to his taste. The west pediment showed Lapiths fighting Centaurs at the wedding of Pirithous in an attempt to win back their ravished womenfolk. The centre of the pediment was dominated by the noble figure of Apollo, god of light and spiritual purity, his hand raised in a lordly gesture as he directed the battle. The Centaurs do not make a monstrous impression, even though they personify the elemental power of bestial urges, unlike the Lapiths, whose physical movements convey athletic agility rather than brute force. The pedimental figures are more than a resplendent memorial to the spirit of athleticism once cultivated at Olympia. Their

113

The Altis with the temple of Zeus, reconstruction by F. Adler (1894).

significance goes still further, because we know that, at the time when the temple of Zeus was built, the subject was intended to symbolize the wars between Greeks and Persians. By unhesitatingly ranging itself on the side of those who were resolved to fight for the freedom of Greece, the Olympian sanctuary had written a glorious page in its long history.

At the Olympic Games of 476 BC Themistocles was jointly honoured by all the Greeks for his victory over the Persians. The votive gift of those who had fought at Plataea was erected and weapons captured 'from the Medes' were displayed in the stadium according to custom. Thus, the Greeks' struggle with the Persians was also expressive of national and athletic tradition as a whole.

Small bronze statues were dedicated to Zeus by the faithful from early times. Most of them showed him in his role as the god of thunder, standing erect, sometimes with his attribute, the eagle, in one hand. Phidias' chryselephantine cult-statue of Zeus was one of the seven wonders of the ancient world. This work combined all his characteristics: he sat enthroned, sovereign lord of gods and men, as though – to quote Homer – a twitch of his brows would have sufficed to shake Olympus. It

114

was a brilliant sculptural achievement born of Olympia's centuries-old conception of the supreme god.

The sanctuary came to full architectural fruition in the fourth century BC. First to be built below the Treasuries were the small Metroön (record office) and the so-called 'South-East Building', which has presented archaeologists with many problems.

We know from Pindar that the games still retained their strong association with Pelops in the fifth century BC – so much so that it would have been unthinkable to hold them outside the Altis. The radical change of outlook which enabled the stadium to be shifted during the fourth century BC was very probably linked with the political and moral crisis that arose from the Peloponnesian War between Athens and Sparta. Olympia in those days boasted countless bronze statues of Zeus, or Zanes, financed by fines paid by athletes who had violated the rules, e.g. by bribing an opponent. Respect for Zeus, the god of oaths, and fear of the hero Pelops had long been insufficient to preserve the ideal of the Olympic Games from contamination. Gone were the days when the *polis*, or city-state, could adhere to religious principles. Thus, the games gradually degenerated into a professional contest.

The buildings of the fourth century BC are expressive of this change. The Leonidaeum was a luxurious hotel for officials, erected on a site where previously tents and simple lodgings had met the needs of official guests. The Philippeum, built after the Battle of Chaeronea (338 BC), further underlined the changed character of Olympia: it was and remained a monument to the Macedonian royal family. For the first time, memorials to earthly monarchs appeared where Zeus had once presided alone, save for fellow gods, spirits and heroes.

During the Hellenistic and Roman periods Olympia shared the fate of Greece, only the Altis being spared its many vicissitudes. The Byzantine Emperor Theodosius I brought Olympia's history to an end by banning the games in AD 393. The chryselephantine cult-statue of Zeus may then have been brought to Constantinople, where it was probably destroyed by fire in 475. All that remained of the Olympian temple of Zeus was devastated during the sixth century by a violent earthquake.

JOHN KONDIS

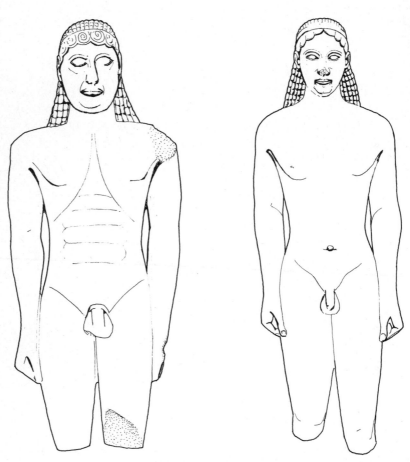

Two typical *kouroi* from the sanctuary of Apollo Ptoios, now in the National Museum, Athens.

The Sanctuaries of Mount Ptoion in Boeotia

In the National Museum at Athens visitors can see a series of nude male statues found in the little-known sanctuary of Apollo Ptoios. In the past only a few people have visited this site in Boeotia, but it can now be reached easily by the national highway N1.

Ptoion is the name of the first mountain in the range which extends eastwards from the Gulf of Euboea. There follow a series of mountains which enclose Lakes Yliki and Paralimni, formed after the drying up of Lake Copais. A narrow mountain track, not easily spotted, leads to the village of Karditsa, now called Akraiphnion in memory of the ancient town Acraephia. The ancient acropolis with its well-preserved sections of wall and Hellenistic towers rises above the main road south of the village. The sanctuary of Apollo is about two miles distant.

Excavations, begun by the French Archaeological Institute under Holleaux in 1884, were discontinued in 1891; work was resumed in 1934-36, and the results were published in the volumes of the *Bulletin de Correspondance Hellénique* for those years and in P. Guillon's book *Les Trépieds du Ptoion* (1943). Parts of the ancient site were later covered by earth washed down the mountainside by rain, and goat-herds drove their flocks into the sanctuary – indeed goats can still be seen grazing there. In 1966 the site underwent cleaning and additional but limited research in furtherance of a publication by Professor J. Ducat.

The sanctuary of Apollo occupies three terraces on the hillside near the spring known as 'Perdikovrisi', a little below the monastery of St Pelagia. It covers an area of some 270 sq. yd. The difference in altitude between the upper and lower terraces is about 130 ft. The temple stood on the highest plateau at an altitude of 1,200 ft; little remains of this Doric temple, 76 × 39 ft, which was entered by way of a deep *pronaos* (vestibule). With thirteen columns of Poros limestone on either side and six at each end, the temple was a *peripteros* (a building with an outer colonnade), but without an *opisthodomos* (chamber at the rear). To judge from column-members, triglyphs, moulding and tiles found on the site, the temple dates from the fourth–third centuries BC and was probably built a little below an earlier wooden temple of the seventh century. A sixth-century tile painted with a Gorgon's head suggests that the wooden temple may have had a ceramic facing, and it is likely that at about this time (probably under the Pisistratids) wooden structural members were replaced with stone. The interest with which prominent Athenians regarded the sanctuary can be gauged from votive offerings presented by a member of the Alcmaeonid family and his younger rival Hipparchus, son of Pisistratus. The bases of these lost votive gifts can be seen in Thebes Museum.

An open space in front of the temple, surrounded by altars, consecrated tripods and plinths for statues, may also have been used for athletic contests. Discovered near by were the *kouroi*, figures of naked youths, which are now displayed in the National Museum at Athens and in Thebes Museum. These finds were the first evidence of Boeotia's prominent role in the development of Archaic art.

The National Museum possesses thirteen sculptures from the Ptoion: first the *kouroi*, which are life-size or somewhat smaller; further, a few heads and female statuettes which must have served as supports for a water-basin; and, finally, the earliest find, a headless statue in a long chiton which may represent Apollo playing the cithara. The latter bears an inscription dating from 620 BC. The more recent statues are dated a century later. Thebes Museum displays three large and three smaller *kouroi*, also heads and fragments of other specimens.

In her book *Kouroi* (1942), Gisela Richter classified these figures by chronological and stylistic criteria. The earliest works in local marble have a stiff and ungainly air. Transitions are so abrupt as to render the figures angular – rugged as the Boeotians themselves, who were farmers closely wedded to the land. Boeotian sculptors soon began to imitate Ionian and Attic works, though not always successfully.

East of the 'square' in front of the temple is a cave hewn into the rock. This contained a spring whose waters once gave inspiration to the divine oracle. Evidently, oracular utterances were made here, and not, as at

Kouros from the sanctuary.
National Museum, Athens.

Delphi, in the temple. An inscription of the third century BC, together
with a votive inscription to Apollo Ptoios, refers to the god as *ennychos,*
which could mean that his advice was sought at night or in darkness –
i.e. inside the cave; no description of the soothsaying ritual exists.
Herodotus (VIII, 135) relates that en envoy from the Persian general
Mardonius, Mys by name, visited the oracle of Apollo Ptoios in quest of
advice. He was accompanied by three Thebans whose task it was to
escort him to the oracle and write the god's reply on a tablet, but much

to their dismay, the oracle-giver couched his pronouncement 'in a barbarian tongue'. Mys snatched the tablet and wrote down the words which were, he said, spoken in the language of Caria. This story recurs, with variations, in Plutarch and Pausanias, who travelled from Thebes to Acraephia but did not actually visit the sanctuary of Apollo Ptoios.

The problem of the 'barbarian tongue' is a bone of contention among archaeologists. Some have inferred from this anecdote that the 'barbarian-speaking oracle' was under Theban rule in 480–479 BC. Evidence for the years prior to 500 BC is lacking, but Herodotus, Pausanias and Strabo state that the sanctuary had always belonged to the Thebans. The Thebans would naturally have attached importance to control of the sanctuary because they feared Thessalian attack and Mount Ptoion commanded the only route from Thermopylae and the coast of Locris. The temple was probably destroyed by the Macedonians in 335 BC, at the same time as Thebes, and rebuilt in 316 BC by Cassander. During the closing years of the fourth century votive gifts from the Boeotian Confederacy were also presented to Apollo Ptoios.

The lowest terrace is supported by two retaining walls, straight on the north side and curved on the south. The sanctuary derives its monumental appearance from the large polygonal stones with which they are faced. Between them is a rectangular cistern divided into six chambers. The French Archaeological Institute has recently cleared the mud from two of these chambers, revealing the slabs of clay which form their floors. An aperture permitted access for cleaning purposes. Like the temple, the cistern dates from 316 BC. Water was carried by conduit to another building which probably had medical and oracular functions. The excavated sections date back to the sixth century. A fountain with a circular basin completed the structure. A clay conduit of more recent date indicates that attempts were made at various stages to canalize the local water-supply, which was plentiful. On the middle terrace, a paved walk led between two parallel colonnades. Further ruins discovered there have yet to be identified.

The local games, or Ptoia, took place every four years in the sanctuary of Apollo. Although they never acquired a pan-Hellenic reputation they continued until the third century BC. The great patron of learning, Herodes Atticus (101–177), was the sanctuary's benefactor, and the inhabitants of Acraephia honoured him by erecting a statue of his daughter Elpinice Regilla.

Today, local inhabitants assemble every summer at the spring of Perdikovrisi to celebrate the festival of St Paraskevi and drink the waters of the spring, which have not lost their curative properties.

Some archaeologists believe that the hero Ptoios was worshipped in the area of Perdikovrisi and that his cult was displaced when that of Apollo gained the upper hand; the inhabitants of Acraephia are thought to have continued to honour their hero by erecting the new sanctuary (excavated in 1903) which lies somewhat further to the west at Kastraki, between Acraephia and Perdikovrisi. This would mean that there were two sanctuaries of the same name and only a thousand yards apart, although existing local cults tended as a rule to be absorbed by those of more important deities. The earliest finds from the Kastraki sanctuary do not, however, antedate 580 BC, whereas the inscription on the cithara-playing Apollo in the National Museum at Athens confirms that Apollo presided over Perdikovrisi as early as 620 BC. J. Ducat thus rejects the theory that the hero Ptoios was worshipped in the Perdikovrisi sanctuary before Apollo, also the view that the Kastraki cult possessed a strictly local character. He cites two items of corroborative evidence: first, that votive offerings from the Boeotians to their hero have been found at Kastraki; and, secondly, that an inscription of 500 BC proves that the inhabitants of Acraephia continued to make votive offerings to the god of Perdikovrisi. It is evident that, after the construction of the second sanctuary at Kastraki, two places of worship existed: the temple and altar on the upper terrace and, lower down, the shrine and altar of the hero.

The lower sanctuary belonged exclusively to the hero Ptoios, as witness the male idols and sixth- and fifth-century vases dedicated to him. Here on the rocky plateau was the *heroön* or actual site of the hero's cult.

A sacred way began in Acraephia and led to the sanctuary. Archaeologists have found rectangular stone bases, each with four recesses – a large one in the centre to take a stone column and three smaller ones for the legs of a bronze cauldron which were often as much as 6–7 ft high. Now exhibited in Thebes Museum, the stone columns bear inscriptions of particular epigraphic interest. Lead – traces of which can still be detected

Reconstruction of stone columns supporting bronze cauldrons.

on them – was used to affix the tripods, whose value and religious purport have been exhaustively studied by Guillon. They were intended to convey the power of the sanctuary and, possibly, to indicate the continuing existence of an oracle in the hero's shrine. The origin of such tripods is lost in myth, like that of the cult itself.

Archaeological discoveries enable us to trace the sanctuary's development in historical times. The small items of bronze in the National Museum of Athens testify to Boeotia's wealth in the sixth century BC. Obviously, large bronze statues were also dedicated to the hero Ptoios. The sixth century was succeeded by the poverty of the fifth and the twilight sleep of the fourth under Theban domination. Kastraki has yielded few finds dating from after the fourth century BC. After the downfall of Thebes, the sanctuary of Apollo at Perdikovrisi probably passed into Acraephian control. Marble statues were dedicated there in the days´of Alexander the Great, during the re-establishment of the Boeotian Confederacy, and into Nero's time.

Of the Doric temple which occupied the topmost terrace at Kastraki, a peripteral structure (30 × 65 ft) enclosed by 8 × 13 columns, only the substructure has survived. The terrace foundations, built of polygonal blocks of local limestone, are impressive. The temple had a deep *pronaos* (vestibule) with columns and a cella divided into two parts by more columns, but no *opisthodomos* (a vestibule at the opposite end, but without access to the cella). Visible today are six large rectangular plinths which supported the wooden columns of the earlier temple dating from the sixth century BC. Sphinx's wings from a facing-tile and other ceramic objects come from the older temple. The ruins that can be seen today date from the fourth or third centuries, as witness column-members, triglyphs, moulding and tiles. A certain air of asymmetry is accounted for by the confined space within which the temple and large rectangular altar were constructed.

The temple was destroyed *c*. 335 BC, probably by the Macedonians. When Cassander restored Thebes' position, however, the Ptoion cult revived and the temple was rebuilt. During this period, therefore, the sanctuary of Apollo Ptoios at Perdikovrisi and that of the hero Ptoios at Kastraki shared a similar fate.

Small female idols of the sixth–fourth centuries BC were discovered near the temple at Kastraki. It was thought that the hero must have been jointly worshipped with a female deity, possibly his mother Zeuxippe (or Euxippe), an earth-goddess, or perhaps a mother-goddess to whom the animal figures – most of them swine – were dedicated. It may also be that, at the Perdikovrisi shrine of Apollo, the god was in ancient times worshipped alongside a nymph whose place was later taken by Athena Pronaia. Her own sanctuary has not been found, but its existence is attested by plinth inscriptions and articles of bronze. Couples of this kind (nymph and hero) were worshipped at other Boeotian sanctuaries.

From these and other elements common to Boeotian sanctuaries (mountainous or spring-fed sites, interpreters of oracular pronouncements), some scholars (e.g. Schachter) have inferred the existence of a tribe which came from Epirus to Boeotia and Phocis during the eighth century BC. Nevertheless, these features are universally found in pre-Hellenic cults from northern Greece to Crete.

EVI TOULOUPA

Reconstruction of figures in the so-called temple of Themis, showing statues of Themis, the priestess of Nemesis, Arsinoë, and boy. The figures are now in the National Museum, Athens.

Rhamnus : on the Track of Nemesis

At Rhamnus, on the north-east coast of Attica, Nemesis was more then a mere embodiment of retribution; she developed into a goddess and was worshipped as such. The sculptor Agoracritus, the favourite pupil of Phidias, produced a colossal statue of the goddess in the fifth century BC. This statue was destroyed and only a few fragments were found by the first excavators of the site in 1812—so few indeed that Agoracritus' masterpiece was generally thought to have been lost for ever. In 1971, however, a young scholar, George Despinis, produced a highly convincing reconstruction of the statue of Nemesis from over three hundred fragments scattered in the store rooms of the Rhamnus museum and the Athens Archaeological Museum—a feat which must surely rank as one of the most brilliant in the history of Greek archaeology. These fragments have now all been gathered together in the Athens museum.

On a terrace high above the sea lie the ruins of the marble temple of Nemesis. The temple, whose cella (great hall) once housed Agoracritus' statue, was enclosed by 6 × 12 Doric columns which formed a covered ambulatory measuring 37 × 75 ft. Today, only the substructure and seven column-members still stand, surrounded by countless truncated columns, bright fragments of marble amid the green undergrowth. Beside the temple of Nemesis stand the walls of the House of Themis, a temple constructed of large polygonal stones, 5–7 ft high, and furnished with a vestibule. It is said to have been partly burned down during the Persian Wars (fifth century BC) but continued to serve as a shrine until it was eventually used as a store-room. Here reigned the goddess Themis, guardian of justice and regulator of the Olympian world order, co-owner of Nemesis' temple precinct and, like her, a guarantor of ordered human existence. The remains of an altar, a cistern, the wall of an ambulatory and two unfinished female statues are all that survive of human handiwork at Rhamnus.

In spring the hills of Rhamnus are bathed in hues of warm rust-red, mustard-yellow and bright green; in summer they turn grey-brown. The commonest form of vegetation is *Rhamnus* (buckthorn), the shrub which gave its name to the district in ancient times, and which was sacred to Nemesis. Its berries yielded a remedy for snake-bite and its branches were used to guard houses against evil spirits in time of birth or sickness. The Nemesites stone, used to conjure up the souls of the dead, is no longer in evidence at Rhamnus, but it is known to have existed just as we know from a third-century list of victors that torch-races used to be run in the goddess's honour. These, too, were often associated with death-cults. Nemesis had a variety of associations with the dead (she was believed to represent those who revisit the earth to plague the living).

Inscriptions (*CIA* 3, 691 and the Megacles Inscription) indicate that, apart from torch-races and athletic contests for men and boys, comedies were probably performed at Rhamnus at the close of a festival associated with sacrifice. The marble statue of a boy named Lysiclides (identified as a competitor in the torch-race) found in the temple of Themis is now in the National Museum at Athens.

One can imagine how, on the eve of the festival in honour of the goddess, the temples glowed with torch-light as priestesses made sacrifice, and how, with the coming of daylight, the eerie spell faded away and crowds assembled for a popular festival, a *paneghiris* of the kind familiar in Greece today. Scholars have so far ascertained relatively few details about the cult of Nemesis. As Tournier wrote in 1863: 'Her cult consisted in the fact that she preyed on people's minds.' There was a cult of Nemesis at Patrae (Peloponnese), at Epidaurus, at Mylassa in Thrace, and at Smyrna in Asia Minor, where two such goddesses were venerated. The sanctuaries at Smyrna and Rhamnus were regarded as the oldest and most important.

On the way down to the sea, ten minutes' walk from the sanctuary, the ancient town of Rhamnus still stands on a hill between two small bays, facing the lofty mountains of Euboea. It was still a popular summer resort in the second century A D. The wealthy sophist Herodes Atticus (101–177), who spent his holidays at Rhamnus, erected a statue of his

Statue of Themis from the temple of Themis. National Museum, Athens.

127

daughter there. Local Greek peasants have for the past two hundred years referred to the fortress of Rhamnus as 'Jews' castle' because Jews or gipsies took refuge there, as they did in many other deserted forts. One can still see massive walls, the remains of a theatre complete with priest's chair, ruined buildings and a large gateway.

Leaving the seaside town and returning to the sanctuary, one skirts the cliff by a steep track which ascends through undergrowth to the rocky terrace above. In the temple of Nemesis, Herodes Atticus dedicated a statue of his deceased pupil Polydeucion 'with whom he had often made sacrifice to the goddess'. The inscription states that it was dedicated by Herod the general and not Herod the scholar, in which capacity he was better known. Nemesis was believed to enforce adherence to the rules of war. The Athenians certainly espoused this theory at the Battle of Marathon (490 BC), when they believed that she was fighting on their side against the Persians. According to a legend recorded by Pausanias, the Persians were so confident that nothing could prevent their conquest of Athens that they landed at Marathon with a block of Parian marble intended for their triumphal monument. This was the very block of marble used for the statue of Nemesis, in which the Greeks saw a stone image of retribution of the Persians' *hubris* (arrogance). Pausanias describes it as follows: 'On her head she wears a wreath entwined with stags and small figures of Nike. In her left hand she holds an apple branch, in her right a bowl . . .'

The relief-adorned base of this statue by Agoracritus is displayed in the National Museum, Athens, and a fragment of its head, 16½ in. high, has been on display in the British Museum, London, since 1820. The lofty brow is surmounted by wavy hair.

In his *Naturalis Historia* Pliny the Elder states that Agoracritus of Paros produced a statue of Aphrodite in a competition with the Athenian sculptor Alcamenes. The biased Athenians awarded the prize to their fellow citizen, whereupon Agoracritus sold his statue on condition that it did not remain in Athens: he renamed it Aphrodite Nemesis, and it was erected at Rhamnus. Pliny's story implies that Nemesis was originally conceived and portrayed as Aphrodite; in other words, *retribution appeared in the guise of perfect beauty*. Did the Athenians of the classical period see beauty and love as the real instrument of retribution? When other gods

Fragment of the head of Nemesis by Agoracritus, now in the British Museum, London; and reconstruction of the head.

wished to punish blood guilt or crime it was more usual for them to make use of the black-clad, awe-inspiring Furies, the spirits of revenge and remorse.

The statement that Agoracritus derived inspiration for the reliefs on the base of his Rhamnusian Nemesis from the (lost) epic poem *Cypria* points in a similar direction. These epics, which in part relate the events leading to the aftermath of the Trojan War, contain a story to the effect that Zeus wished to decimate mankind because the earth was overpopulated. He consulted Themis, custodian of 'world order', who referred him to Nemesis. Zeus became enamoured of Nemesis and pursued her over land and sea. He eventually caught up with her at Rhamnus, where they mated, he in the shape of a swan and she in that of a goose. The result was the legendary egg of vengeance, which Leda found 'among blue hyacinths', or which Nemesis dropped into her lap. The egg produced Helen, quintessence of feminine beauty and immediate cause of the Trojan War. Thus, a lovely woman became the instrument with which Zeus decimated mankind.

Finally, the apple branch which Agoracritus' Nemesis held in her left hand was also an attribute of Aphrodite. This could perhaps have signified that, as Pausanias says, Nemesis 'is most potent in love'. Courtesans and prostitutes invoked not only Aphrodite but Nemesis as well. The Greeks, who specialized in drawing up genealogies establishing relationships between gods and heroes, old and young, local and imported, made sisters of Aphrodite and Nemesis. Aphrodite was the senior goddess of destiny and, as such, sister to Nemesis and the Furies. They were born of the drops of blood that fell from Uranus, who had been castrated by his son Kronos. Another genealogy makes Nemesis the venerable mother of Erechtheus, the legendary king of Athens. Erechtheus honoured his mother by founding a sanctuary at Rhamnus, her birthplace.

At this period, long before young Agoracritus of Paros sculpted his statue of the goddess, Nemesis merely personified certain ideas and concepts: the power which punished and took vengeance on all immoderation and *hubris*, and divine envy of excessive human good fortune. An attempt was made to derive the name Nemesis from *nemein* (dispense) and construe it as 'she who dispenses what is due'.

As the years went by, every Greek god acquired many different capacities in addition to his original function, a process which led to such confusion in Hellenistic times that Lucian, in his *Theon Ecclesia*, causes Momos (the mythological personification of criticism) to say that the lords of Olympus ought kindly to decide which of them would heal, prophesy, protect cities or promote fertility. Athena, for example, should concentrate on Athens, which would still give her more than enough to do; she really had no need to play the oculist as well.

Although Nemesis does not fall into this category, she has been an object of special interest to poets, philosophers, theologians, historians and philologists. In Homer she appears as moral awareness. In Hesiod she is the 'affliction-bringing daughter of Night', sister to Affection (*philotes*), Treachery (*apate*), Destiny (*moros*), Sleep (*hypnos*), Death (*thanatos*), Age (*geras*), Strife (*eris*) and Censure (*momos*). In his poem *Works and Days* Hesiod makes Nemesis leave the earth with Aidos (shame and modesty) when the Iron Age of man is born, in other words, when sacrilege gains ground. Pindar sees her as a power who attends to the fulfilment of justice among mortals. In Herodotus we find Nemesis, as representative of the gods, chastising the Lydian king Croesus for *hubris* (he considered himself the most fortunate of men); after the battle of Marathon she punished the Persian king Xerxes, his children and children's children. Plato states in his *Laws* (*Nomoi* 717) that children have a duty to cherish their parents in old age, just as the latter have unselfishly nourished and reared them in the past. This first and earliest debt must be repaid – 'Nemesis, the messenger of Justice, watches over all such things.' To Aristotle, Nemesis is a concept mid-way between envy (*phthonos*) and malicious pleasure. In Pausanias (1, 33, 2) she appears as the avenger of *hubris*. She was especially feared by those who had neglected to revere the gods and respect their parents. In his tragedy *Electra*, Sophocles makes Clytemnestra believe that her son Orestes has been punished by Nemesis for such sentiments (l. 793). Orestes' sister Electra, in her turn, summons Nemesis to listen to their mother's words of loathing as she exults over Orestes' supposed death. Scorn for another's misfortune brings misfortune to the author of that scorn. 'But divine retribution falls not on him that kills a tyrant,' wrote Theognis.

In his comedy *Nemesis*, which was staged in Athens in 429 BC and has survived only in fragmentary form, Cratinus parodies the Rhamnusian cult-legend by representing Pericles as Zeus the swan and Aspasia as Nemesis the goose. From their union, i.e. their political machinations, springs the fateful egg – in this case the Peloponnesian War – which is hatched out on stage by Spartan Leda.

In Nonnus, a late classical poet, Nemesis for the first time chastises with her own hand, something which she has evidently not done before. Modern philologists conclude that Nemesis originally, and for a long time, personified the threat of retribution rather than its actual fulfilment; that she was a deity who required men to be on their guard at all times.

The word *nemesis* still figures in the Greek vocabulary, and has been adopted in others; the idea which it represents is part of everyday life, even though the Greeks no longer place their fourth finger on their lips and then on the so-called 'place of Nemesis' behind the ear, for fear of having tempted providence by some chance remark – an ancient custom referred to by Pliny the Elder.

EVI MELAS

The plain of Sparta with the Taygetus range beyond.

The Spartan Sanctuary of Artemis Orthia

Ancient Peloponnesian tradition claimed that the mythical ancestor of the Lacedaemonians, the hero Lacedaemon, was a son of Zeus and the Nymph Taygete whom he had ravished. Taygete gave her name to the massif which forms a barrier between the Laconian valley and Arcadia and Messenia. She gave birth to the much-sung Eurotas, the river whose course crosses the plain of Sparta. Taygete's story recalls the type of fate which befell all the loves of Zeus: she fled from him, was transformed by Artemis into a hind, pursued by the goddess of the chase and captured by Heracles. After regaining her original shape, Taygete is said to have dedicated the hind to Artemis Orthia.

Legends such as these sought to trace the Spartans' ancestry back to the gods and personify their links with the district. They also drew attention to the intimate ties between Sparta and Artemis Orthia, who was one of the city's tutelary deities from prehistoric times until its final destruction. Her cult was expressive of a singular religious approach which accorded with Spartan principles and institutions, and her sanctuary was a centre of State education.

The cult-legend relates that Artemis Orthia arrived in Sparta during Homeric times, when tidings of 'gold-rich' Mycenae preceded the Dorian migration, i.e. c. 1100 BC. It was believed that Orestes and Iphigenia had carried off the wooden image of Artemis Orthia from barbarian Tauris, although other places, notably Brauron (cf. p. 49) in Attica, also laid claim to the original cult-statue. Orestes was supposed to have brought it to Sparta when he married Hermione, daughter of Menelaus and Helen, and became king of Sparta. According to the most common version of the legend, the wooden image reputed to have come from Tauris was discovered centuries later, concealed in a chaste tree (*Vitex agnus castus*). Artemis duly acquired the epithet 'Orthia' (Upright), because the branches of the bush had held her statue erect. This is the simplest of the numerous versions of the myth, born of the endeavour to find an etymological explanation of the surname. Another explanation is that Artemis became amalgamated with an earlier goddess named Orthia. Finally, some authorities derive the epithet from *orthros* (dawn).

The story of Iphigenia in Tauris recalls the sacrifice at Aulis. When Agamemnon proposed to sacrifice his daughter to appease the gods, the latter demonstrated that human sacrifice was not invariably the right answer. Memories of the abolition of human sacrifice were classically expressed in Euripides' *Iphigenia in Tauris*. One wonders if the Athenians who first saw this tragedy in 414 BC realized that Euripides had here furnished Artemis with the ideals of the classical age. The Attic sanctuaries of Artemis exemplified the humanization which Euripides had illustrated in his tragedy. They remained in sharp contrast to the Spartan cult of Artemis until the end of classical antiquity.

It seems positively fateful that so many stone relics of the Athenians' cults should have survived, whereas the monuments which Sparta erected to its gods were completely destroyed. Today the sparse remains of the temple of Athena Chalkioikos are hard to detect in the vast expanse of ruins that used to be the acropolis of Sparta. The acropolis itself is now dominated by the grey mass of the Roman theatre, which tells us more about the period of Sparta's decline than about its Archaic and classical renown. The modern town of Sparta was designed – like the new Athens – in a spirit of romanticism. This finally destroyed the remains of the celebrated temple of Artemis and of Dionysus Kolonatas, also the agora (market-place) with its 'Persian colonnade', constructed from spoils taken in the Persian Wars.

Confronted by the ruins of the temple of Artemis Orthia, one finds it hard to visualize the sanctuary's ancient splendour. The Eurotas is fringed by tall eucalyptus trees, and the ancient name of this district – Limnes or Limnaia (marshland) – is an allusion to the river's habit of overflowing. Flood-water from the Eurotas, which has since changed its course, still represents a threat during the rainy months of winter. The waters of the river partly destroyed the sanctuary, which sustained additional damage from violent earthquakes and was eventually devastated by the Goths under Alaric in AD 396, when ancient Sparta's history came to an end.

Reconstruction of the sanctuary of Artemis Orthia in Roman times.

The ruins now visible at the site all date from the sanctuary's final phase, i.e. the third century A D. The temple was small (55 × 25 ft) in relation to the altar (27 ft × 8 ft 6 in.) and the amphitheatre (diameter 177 ft). The sanctuary's earliest relics date from the tenth century B C. Only the temple's foundations have survived. The ruins of the large altar and amphitheatre lie to the east. About 1000 B C the sanctuary consisted of a detached plot reserved for the goddess, to whom a small altar was built. The remains of an altar dating from the ninth century B C were found in front of the large Archaic altar. The sanctuary did not assume monumental form until the eighth century, when a temple was erected on stone foundations, its roof supported by an interior colonnade. The pediment showed lions dismembering a bull, a motif frequently found in other Archaic temples. Some modest limestone reliefs enable us to reconstruct the appearance of the Archaic temple, which was destroyed c. 600 B C by a flood. A new temple built of the same material underwent repairs in the fifth and fourth centuries; its remains can still be seen today. Xenocles' votive stele of the second century B C appears to show it after renovation.

Excavation of the sanctuary of Artemis Orthia has failed to determine whether the Roman amphitheatre was preceded by an earlier building. It is probable that a man-made rampart of earth served as a stand from which spectators could observe the rites. A large number of clay masks were unearthed here, and it has been concluded from a study of them that from the seventh century BC onwards, if not earlier, ritual dances were performed round the goddess's altar. The masks were provided with two holes so that they could be suspended, a feature which betrays their cult origin, and represent mythological figures, satyrs, sileni – wrinkled old men – and faces with elements of portraiture, occasionally idealized and sometimes terrifying. Their purpose seems to have been to spare their donors the misfortune they symbolized. The fact that they were hung up, not worn, suggests that they were replicas of wooden or leather masks used in the ritual dance. Dorian settlers in Italy performed similar dances with wooden masks in honour of Artemis Corythalia.

Alcman, a poet who lived in Sparta *c.* 680 BC, confirms the tradition that ancient cult-dances were performed in the sanctuary of Artemis Orthia. His celebrated cult-song 'Parthenion' speaks of dances by maidens who bring the goddess a springtime gift. Some scholars believed that this was a robe of the sort used in the Attic sanctuary of Artemis at Brauron, others that the Spartan girls dedicated a plough and the boys a sickle, ritual gifts presented to Artemis Orthia in her role as a fertility-goddess. Still others took the view that the maidens of Sparta brought Orthia a symbolic gift which Alcman's song left undefined so as to preserve the mystical nature of the festivities. What is certain is that the sanctuary of Artemis Orthia did, from ancient times, witness acts of worship – dramatic rites which never developed into theatrical performances proper, as in Athens.

One series of ritual acts is especially interesting because of its direct association with the controversial subject of Spartan education. Under Spartan law, parents were responsible for their children only until the age of seven. After that, the *polis* (city-state) took over their education. During the first six years of State education, boys were divided by age-groups into *agelai* (herds) and given gymnastic and military instruction by a somewhat older youth. They were trained to withstand severe physical stress, control their bodies and toughen their characters. Obedience and respect were instilled into them, also a code of honour and sense of tradition which stifled all progressive tendencies and doubts. The ideal soldier – one who devoted his entire life to the State – was deliberately created here. The course of State education culminated in a series of contests at the sanctuary of Artemis Orthia. Victors were awarded an iron sickle which they subsequently dedicated on a marble stele in the goddess's sanctuary. We learn from inscriptions found on numerous stelae that there were three main types of contest: a race and two competitions, one in singing and the other in declamation.

Older Spartan youths were obliged to take part in a special annual contest, a test of endurance which earned the cult a reputation all its own: they were flogged before the goddess's altar and victory went to the youth who endured most punishment. In Roman times this practice not infrequently resulted in the death of aspiring ephebes; parents and spectators from distant cities would cheer the youngsters on and threaten those who showed signs of weakness. Plutarch wrote in the first century A D: 'The boys who are flogged all day on the altar of Artemis Orthia often remain blithe and cheerful unto death; they vie with each other to see which of them can best and longest endure the blows. The victor is held in the highest esteem . . .'

The cult-statue of Artemis Orthia seems to have resembled a column, with its arms held close to its sides. Tradition relates that a priestess held it erect beside the altar while scourging was in progress. Though small and light, the wooden image is said to have weighed ever heavier in the priestess's hands as soon as the flogging diminished in severity – perhaps out of pity for some handsome youth. This, allegedly, was the goddess's way of conveying that she wanted no pity shown. Only plain marble bases can now be seen in the museum at Sparta. The bronze statues of the victors in this singular contest have disappeared.

Pausanias, who visited Sparta during the second century A D and listed many useful topographical particulars, believed that ritual flogging had replaced the human sacrifices of earlier times. Human sacrifice as a form of atonement and purification intended to promote fertility of the soil, the origin and end of all things, is far more reminiscent of an earth-dwelling Artemis than of a mountain-roaming goddess of the chase. Artemis Orthia recalls the figure of the Great Goddess of the matriarchal past, bestower of life and death and mistress of the animal world. It is strange that the Spartans, who always prided themselves on their pure Dorian descent, should have venerated this indubitably pre-Hellenic goddess.

A. DELIVORRIAS

The mouth of the Acheron on the gulf of Ammoudia.

The Oracle of the Dead on the Acheron

It is the sorceress Circe – so Homer tells us in the tenth book of the
Odyssey (l. 487 ff.) – who advises Odysseus to descend into the underworld, there to ask the blind seer Tiresias his homeward route to Ithaca.
In due course, Homer goes on, Odysseus' ship will be carried by the
north wind to a desolate coast at the extremity of Oceanus, where stands
the 'untouched grove' of Persephone. After he has landed, Odysseus'
journey to Hades will bring him to a spot where the rivers Pyriphlegethon
and Cocytus, the latter gushing from the Styx, meet the Acheron with a
mighty, tumultuous roar. Marking the spot is a cavern surmounted by a
rock. Having dug a pit less than a cubit wide, Odysseus will pour into it
honey and milk, then sweet wine and water, and finally flour, as an
offering to the dead. That done, he will supplicate the shades of the dead,
promising them and Tiresias two beasts from his herd as soon as he has
returned home: the finest black ram and a barren cow, also black.
Thereafter, keeping his own eyes fixed on the river, he must slaughter a
ram and a sheep above the pit. His companions shall skin and burn the
beasts, likewise supplicating the souls of the departed. The dead will
then rise in a whirling throng to partake of the blood and offerings.
Odysseus may, however, hold them at bay with his sharp sword until
Tiresias' shade has drunk first and foretold the adventures that will befall
him on his homeward voyage.

In the eleventh book of the *Odyssey*, Odysseus reaches the edge of
Oceanus where lie the country and citadel of the Cimmerians, eternally
sunless and wreathed in cloud. Taking a few companions and his offerings, he comes to the place described by the sorceress Circe. All are
deeply grieved and 'their eyes filled with tears'. They do as Circe has
advised. There then appear youths and maidens lamenting their untimely
death, greybeards bowed with sorrow, men in armour still red with the

The east side of the hill with the 18th century church on the site of the ancient oracle.

blood of battle; but first Tiresias drinks and makes utterance ...
Homer's dramatic description is the earliest and most detailed account of
a hero's descent into Hades.

Others travelled there too, among them Orpheus, who sought, found
and again lost his beloved Eurydice, and Heracles, who planned to bring
to King Eurystheus the unsleeping guardian of the underworld, Cer-
berus, a monstrous three-headed dog.

Homer's description of the entrance to the underworld may be poetic
but is not devoid of topographical accuracy. Excavations conducted by
the Greek Archaeological Society and myself have unearthed the probable
Homeric site. This is situated in the western part of Epirus in north-west
Greece, in Thesprotia, barely 2½ miles from the Ionian coast, in a plain
which as recently as twenty years ago was still covered by the marshy
remains of Lake Acherusia. The marshes have since been drained and the
whole of the picturesque plain is fertile. No one would guess that the
Lake of the Dead once brooded there. Near Mesopotamon, at the con-

140

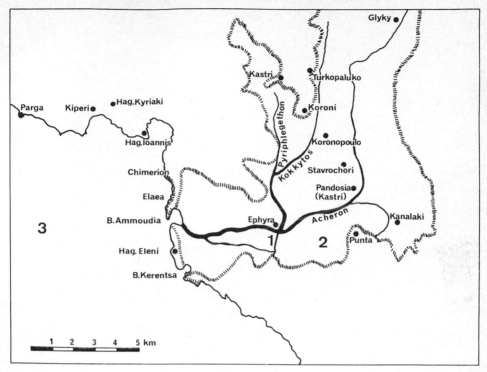

Map of the area showing: 1, Oracle of the Dead near Ephyra; 2, Lake Acherusia; 3, Ionian Sea.

fluence of the Cocytus (Kokkytos) and Acheron, stands a rocky hill; the small monastery built at its summit during the eighteenth century was superimposed on the ancient ruins of the Oracle of the Dead. A little over two miles to the west, the Acheron flows into the Bay of Ammoudia, known in ancient times as 'Glycys Limen' (sweet harbour) on account of the fresh water discharged into it by the Acheron.

Exploration of the district revealed that a hill six hundred yards north of the Oracle of the Dead harboured the remains of Ephyra, a very ancient city. Thucydides, who describes the area with characteristic attention to detail (1, 46, 3–4), localizes the city of Ephyra, the river Acheron and Lake Acherusia. Furthermore, Ephyra is also mentioned in

141

legends relating to the mouth of Hades. Theseus tried to abduct Perse-phone, 'spouse of Aedoneus, King of Ephyra', but he and his friend Pirithous were kept in chains by Aedoneus until rescued by Heracles. The king's name was synonymous with Hades and the oracle sacred to Hades was only five hundred yards from his city. It is clear, therefore, that legend was correct in siting the entrance to Hades close to Ephyra. The city's Cyclopean walls, together with other archaeological finds, confirm that Ephyra was a Mycenaean foundation of the fourteenth century BC colonized by settlers from the Western Peloponnese.

Particulars supplied by Thucydides and Strabo agree that the river Acheron flowed into lake Acherusia and that, when the water-level was high, it joined the Cocytus in finding a common outlet near Ephyra in the bay of Glycys Limen. A rocky ridge there was known as 'Chimerion'. Bearing in mind that the banks of the Acheron were clothed in the very trees mentioned by Homer in his account of Perse-phone's 'untouched grove', and that, as in the *Odyssey*, two rivers have their confluence near a tall rock, we can take it that Homer's description refers to the Acheron and its environs. As for the 'Cimmerians', who still lived beside the Black Sea during the eighth century BC and were thus unknown to the Ionian Greeks – Homer included – until the seventh, it seems likely that they were really the 'Chimerians' of Thesprotia (Epirus), who lived on the tongue of land referred to by Thucydides. Homer's topography would thus accord fully with the district near the Acheron. Pausanias (I, 17, 5) confirms this: 'Homer seems to me to have seen this and been bold enough to include it in the remainder of his account of Hades, and even to have borrowed the names of rivers from those in Thesprotia.'

The importance attached to the Thesprotian oracle of the dead in ancient times is underlined by an anecdote in Herodotus (v, 92). The historian tells how in the sixth century BC Periander, tyrant of Corinth, sent envoys to the oracle of the dead beside the Acheron to ask the shade of his wife Melissa, whom he had murdered, where she had hidden some valuables belonging to a friend. Melissa appeared to the envoys but declined to give them any information because she was 'unclad and cold'. The avaricious Periander had, in fact, violated funerary custom by cremating his wife's body while retaining her clothes and jewellery. Only when he had invited the beauties of Corinth to a feast and bidden them sacrifice their own finery was Melissa sufficiently appeased to divulge what was asked of her.

Ancient written sources describe the perils attendant on encounters with the dead. Alcestis, whom Heracles brought back from the underworld to the land of the living, required three days of 'purification' (*katharmos, aphagnismos*) in order to dispel the pollution (*miasma*) of death and regain consciousness (Euripides, *Alcestis*, 1, 145-6). After murdering his wife's suitors in the palace of Ithaca, Odysseus burnt sulphur there in order to cleanse it (*Odyssey*, 22, 481-2; 23, 51).

Ten centuries later, Lucian gives a fascinating account of the physical and mental preparations undertaken by visitors to the oracle of the dead before they made contact with the souls of the departed. Lucian's dialogue *Menippus*, set somewhere between the Euphrates and Tigris, burlesques methods of conjuring up the dead. Despite its note of comedy and satire, his description may be taken to apply to all such practices in the contemporary world. To quote from *Menippus*:

> The magician Mithrobarzanes began by conducting me [Menippus] to the Euphrates every day before sunrise, for a period of twenty-nine days reckoned from the new moon, and there washing me; the while, with his face turned to the east, he recited a long prayer of which I comprehended but little, for he reeled it off in an indistinct and drawling voice. I understood only that he quoted certain daemons by name. This formula complete, he spat thrice in my face and we returned home, I being forbidden to look at anyone on the way. During this time we lived only on walnuts, milk, hydromel [a mixture of honey and water] and water from the river Choaspes, and slept under the sky on an expanse of greensward. After I had been duly prepared by such mortifications, he conducted me at midnight to the Tigris, cleansed me again in water, dried me off and circled me several times holding a pinewood torch, a sea-onion [squill] and sundry other objects, steadfastly muttering a magic formula between his teeth. Having thus magically consecrated me over and over again, he led me home, walking backwards, to prepare for the journey itself. He now donned a magic robe which closely resembled the costume worn by Persian magicians, but me he provided with hat, lion's skin and lyre, bidding me, should anyone inquire my name, to call myself not Menippus but Heracles, Odysseus or Orpheus.

At dawn they travelled down the Euphrates by boat, accompanied by sacrificial sheep, to a marshy spot . . .

> Here we went ashore, the magician walking ahead. Then we dug a pit, slaughtered the sheep and sprinkled the pit all round with sacrificial blood. While the sacrifice was in progress the magician held a burning torch in his hand, and, speaking not in an undertone as heretofore but at the top of his voice, recited the names of all the daemons of the Kingdom of the Dead, conjuring up the avenging spirits and Fates, nocturnal Hecate and stern Persephone, and adding sundry barbaric and polysyllabic names which were wholly unfamiliar to me.

Between 1958 and 1964, excavation of the hill-top beside the confluence of the Acheron and Cocytus brought to light the ancient oracle of the dead, hitherto concealed by the eighteenth-century church and cemetery. A twisting, labyrinthine passage-way measuring some 200 × 150 ft, with an entrance facing north, encloses the sanctuary proper, which is 72 ft square. This structure is divided by two parallel walls into a central chamber and two lateral aisles of which each is split into three chambers by transverse walls. Beneath the central chamber is a subterranean chamber of equal size, hewn into the rock: the 'gloomy palace of Persephone and Hades', the ceiling of which forms the floor of the chamber above.

West of this building extends the sacred precinct, which provided accommodation for priests and visitors, and store-rooms. Leaving their quarters, pilgrims bade farewell to the light of day and made their way down a passage with three gates. On the left of the corridor are three chambers, of which the third was furnished with a bath and used for incubation. There in the impenetrable gloom, oracle-seekers consumed pork and special kinds of beans and shellfish, i.e. foodstuffs associated with the dead, and drank milk, honey and water.

The ritual cleansing was accompanied by magic ceremonial: the priest intoned or sang in a mood-inducing manner and addressed unintelligible prayers to the spirits of the nether world. Before the visitor entered the east passage he warded off misfortune by casting a stone on to an existing pile of such stones and entered yet another chamber. We do not know how long he would remain there. The sacred dietary rules became stricter, the magic rituals more frequent, the mood of spiritual exaltation

The main hall of the sanctuary (above), with entrance to the labyrinth, and the Anaktoron (below), the subterranean chamber beneath.

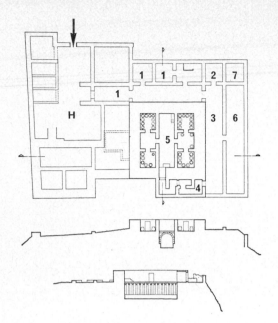

Plan and sections showing: 1, dark passage and chamber; 2, chamber; 3, passage into which sacrificial animals were brought; 4, labyrinthine passage; 5, three-aisled central chamber; 6, east passage chamber; 6, east passage leading to exit; 7, purification chamber. Scale 1 : 80.

Metal objects from the ▶ Oracle of the Dead. Ioannina Museum.

more intense. The species of leguminous plant (related to *Vicia faba equina*) eaten by suppliants, a plant which grew in Thesprotia as it did in Egypt, induced the dizziness, suggestibility and hallucinations which were prerequisites for communion with the dead.

When the crucial moment drew near, communicants were led along the east passage, where sheep were sacrificed in pits. (The remains of charred animal bones were found there during excavations.) From these pits, the visitor's route took him into the labyrinthine south passage, a maze of dark corridors designed to simulate the tortuous paths of the underworld. Clay vessels stood everywhere in this south passage, probably as receptacles for flour and other dry votive offerings. Finally, the visitor passed through the three iron portals of the labyrinth into the main chamber where he cast a stone and poured libations on the floor beneath which lay the 'gloomy palace of Hades'. He had reached his destination, the place where he would encounter the dead.

Among other appurtenances found in the central chamber were a large bronze cauldron and, scattered round it, a number of bronze pulley wheels belonging to an iron machine so constructed that it could raise

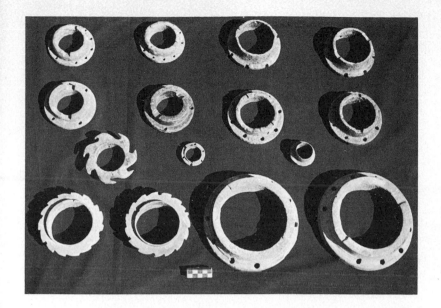

and lower heavy weights. It is clear from the nature of this find and its position in the sanctuary's main chamber, where the shades of the dead were supposed to appear, that it was closely associated with such ghostly apparitions.

The sanctuary was two-storeyed. The exterior walls, being nearly 11 ft thick, provided space for secret passages in which people could move about unobserved. Bronze cauldrons could evidently be raised or lowered by means of the hoist. The Hellenistic era was a time of scientific and intellectual inquiry, so the priests of the oracle of the dead must have been compelled to stage their otherworldly performances with great expertise.

Visitors to the Oracle of the Dead were not permitted to encounter those who came after them, and left the sanctuary by another route. It seems that they emerged through a door in the east interior which led into the exterior passage, and from there into a chamber where they doubtless underwent the ritual purification prescribed for those who had communed with the dead. To judge by traces found in the sanctuary, priests must have burnt sulphur there as Odysseus did after slaying the suitors. Finally discharged, the visitor made his way downhill to the Cocytus, his lips sealed on the subject of all he had seen and heard.

The sanctuary has yielded a profusion of vases, large vessels for the storing of honey and fruit, millstones and iron implements; some date from the fourth century, but most belong to the third or early second century B C. One clay votive gift of the third century portrays Persephone, goddess of the underworld. She wears a tall head-dress (*polos*) adorned with fruit symbolic of fertility. Her dainty countenance conveys the majesty of an underworld deity and the graciousness of a mother-goddess.

Clay figure of Persephone, goddess of the underworld, 3rd century BC.

Vases found at the site of the Oracle, Ionnina Museum.

When the rocky plateau was levelled to allow the construction of the Hellenistic sanctuary unearthed by our excavations, many older relics underlying it were lost for ever. A few prehistoric finds and a Mycenaean grave are all that have come to light.

There is much to be said for the supposition that the cult of Hades antedated Homer's *Odyssey*. It was probably brought to Epirus by Mycenaean migrants from the Western Peloponnese, an area where the cult was widespread and the names Acheron and Ephyra are also found. It is possible, on the other hand, that the Thesproti who settled in Epirus during the second century BC transplanted the cult from there to the Peloponnese. The sanctuary was eventually destroyed by fire in 167 BC, when the Romans conquered Epirus.

S. DAKARIS

View of the sanctuary from the north, showing the new temple of Dione (left), the sacred dwelling-place (centre) and the temple of Themis.

The Sanctuary of Dodona

Heinrich Schliemann's excavations at Troy, which began in 1870, stunned the world with the realization that the Trojan War was not simply a myth, but historical fact. Prompted by Schliemann's example, K. Karapanos decided to seek the shrine of Pelasgian Zeus at Dodona; in 1875, armed with a licence from the Sublime Porte, he started to dig in Epirus, which was then ruled by the Turks. (Dodona occupies a narrow valley 14 miles from the town of Ioannina.)

Homer relates how Odysseus visited this sanctuary during his eventful homeward voyage to inquire of the oracle – a lofty oak – how best to return to his homeland of Ithaca, either openly or incognito, and Hesiod states that Zeus dwelt by the roots of the sacred oak in 'far-off, wintry-bleak Dodona'. The Selli (or Helli), a clan of priests and prophets from whom the Hellenes may have derived their name, lived by it; they slept on the ground and went barefoot and with unwashed feet. The Selli's ascetic way of life and the primitive form of cult which linked them permanently with the forces of earth bespeak the cult's great antiquity. Traces of this rite – relics of an ancient practice – are later encountered in other regions of Greece. When the Argonauts were building their ship the goddess Athena fetched a piece of wood from the sacred oak at Dodona and fitted it into the *Argo*'s bow, giving the vessel a human voice and enabling it to counsel the Argonauts in time of need. The original version of the Argonaut saga does not survive, but the story undoubtedly antedates the *Odyssey*, which refers to it.

Karapanos' excavations at Dodona brought to light votive gifts and inscriptions scratched on thin sheets of lead. It emerges from these that the oldest Greek oracle, referred to by Argonaut saga and Homeric epic alike, actually existed. Fifteen years after Epirus was reunited with Greece, the Greek Archaeological Society began to dig at Dodona. The

Fragments of lead sheet bearing inscriptions, 4th and 3rd century BC; the upper example refers to the completion of a ship built at the behest of Apollo, and appeals for the protection of Zeus, Themis and Dione.

author has supplemented Professor Evangelides' long years of research by excavating and restoring the theatre, Prytaneum (town hall) and Bouleuterion (council chamber). 'So remote' in Homer's day and, according to Hesiod, 'set on the edge of the Greek world', Dodona can today be approached by road without difficulty.

Cut off by the Pindus range, a continuation of the Dinaric Alps, and separated from the commercial and cultural centres of southern Greece, Dodona retained its prehistoric cultural character until the classical period. Ancient Greek mariners who landed on the shores of the Ionian Sea founded a series of colonies there in the Mycenaean period (fourteenth–thirteenth centuries BC) and again in the seventh century BC.

The natives remained politically and culturally 'underdeveloped' and allowed themselves to be exploited by the newcomers. Until the turn of the fifth–fourth century BC they lived in unfortified villages, spoke Greek but could not write it. They had no coinage, only a system of barter: they 'sold' cattle, wood, wine and oil in exchange for merchandise which came to Epirus from north and south, such as wheat, clay vessels made on the potter's wheel, jewellery and cloth. Prices, as in Homer's day, were reckoned in cattle.

The Epirote kings, who (like the Mycenaean rulers) combined military, political and religious power, were sometimes endowed with charismatic

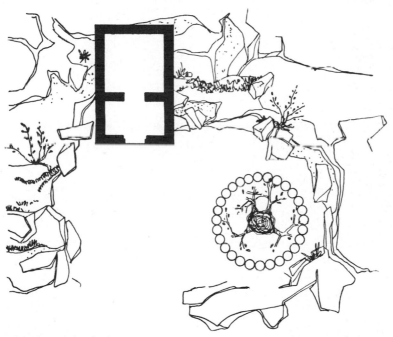

Reconstruction of the dwelling-place of Zeus, with the sacred oak, at the end of the 5th century B.C.

Bronze statuette of Zeus with thunderbolt, *c.* 470 BC, from Dodona. Staatliche Museen, Berlin.

and curative powers as well. One such monarch was the third-century king Pyrrhus. The Peloponnesian War (431–404 BC) wrought substantial changes among the Epirote tribes when the Molossi, the strongest tribe, allied themselves with Athens. Their king, Tharypas (423–385 BC), had spent his childhood in Athens and been profoundly impressed by the democratic ideals prevailing there. Attic culture began to percolate north-west Greece during his reign. The Molossi, who had settled between Thessaly and Dodona in the twelfth century BC, were the main vehicles of this influence. Dodona itself remained in the hands of the ancient Thesproti, and Euripides' *Phoenissae* (first performed in 410 BC) refers to it as 'Thesprotian soil'.

It was not until early in the fourth century BC that Dodona passed to the Molossi, who controlled the whole of Epirus from then onwards. This period represents not only a milestone in the history of Epirus but a turning-point in that of Dodona. Local conservatism had preserved the ancient rites to which urban Greeks of the classical era took such exception: the Selli still slept on the bare ground and went about with unwashed feet.

Dodona looked upon Dione, not Hera, as the consort of Zeus ('Dione' being the feminine form of Zeus). It was believed that the divine pair dwelt, not on Olympus, but in the roots of the sacred oak, or on Mount Tomarus which rises majestically to the west of the valley of Dodona.

What makes the exploration of the sanctuary of Dodona so interesting is that it leads us back to the roots of Greek civilization as it was before southern influence took hold. Detailed study is, however, rendered more difficult by the fact that archaeologists have virtually no philological sources to draw on. Excavation of the sanctuary confirms that, until the end of the fifth century BC, Zeus continued to be worshipped in the open air beneath his sacred oak. A large number of tripods and cauldrons stood round the tree, protecting it. When the bronze cauldrons were struck, their various notes produced a chord from which the Selli interpreted the will of Zeus. Ancient tradition invested such sounds with the power to avert evil. The bronze cauldrons and tripods were not originally instruments of prophecy, therefore, but a form of protection for the abode of Zeus and his consort Dione.

The cult of Zeus at Dodona goes back to the fourteenth–thirteenth centuries BC, if not further. Archaeological research has confirmed what we are told by the Homeric epic and saga of the Argonauts. The exact origin of the cult is unknown; it is uncertain whether the Greek population which migrated to Epirus and settled there brought the cult with them early in the second millennium BC, or whether the cult came from Thessaly, home of the Olympian gods, or whether it travelled north with Mycenaean settlers. Votive offerings in the shape of Mycenaean vases, jewellery and weapons, testify to active contacts between the sanctuary and the Mycenaean world.

One is struck by the earthly elements in this cult of Zeus. The Greek Zeus is no earth-god – he reigns in the heavens, manifests himself in the rain, descends with the lightning, dwells in the aether. At Dodona, however, Zeus had his abode beside the roots of the oak, as Hesiod says, and his priests derived prophetic powers from the soil on which they slept. The temple of this cult evolved in the style of a Greek house, shut off from the outside world like so many sanctuaries. Polybius refers to the temple as 'sacred house', a designation which corresponds with the Erechtheum on the Acropolis at Athens and provides further confirmation that Dodona's was originally a cult associated with the forces of earth.

Zeus of Dodona was additionally called 'Naios' and his consort Dione 'Naia', surnames which have presented philologists with a number of problems. The surname Naios should be related, not to *naiein* (flow) but to *naiein* (dwell, inhabit), a word from which *naos* (abode, temple) also derives. Thus, Naios means the god inhabiting the soil of Dodona, as it does in Hesiod. There the god's earthly presence manifested itself in the rustling of oak leaves. The epithet 'Phegonaios' likewise means the god who dwells in the oak.

In addition, the temple of Zeus was called *hiera oikia* (sacred house), an expression equivalent to the word *naos,* and this we encounter specifically among earth-cults. Many other symbols confirm the nature of the cult at Dodona.

Herodotus (II, 54) recounts an anecdote which he heard from the priests of the sanctuary of Zeus at Thebes in Egypt and likewise at Dodona in Epirus. The Theban version was that, once upon a time, Phoenician pirates abducted two women. One of them they sold in Libya, where she founded the oracle of Zeus Ammon and became its first priestess, and the other in Dodona, where she founded the sanctuary. For their part, the priests of Dodona related that two grey pigeons, not women, had flown from Thebes to the two sanctuaries and founded the oracles there. Herodotus surmises that the Egyptian language sounded like the cooing of a pigeon to the Epirotes, who duly named the foreign woman after the bird; this fact was, however, forgotten by succeeding generations because their priestesses now spoke the vernacular, but the name 'Peleia' lived on.

(a) Epirote bronze coin, reverse depicting three pigeons and the sacred oak of Dodona; (b, c) Silver stater, obverse and reverse depicting Zeus and Dione, and a bull within an oak wreath, 3rd century BC. All Franke Collection, Saarbrücken.

An Epirote bronze coin, dated to the fourth century by Professor Franke, actually portrays three pigeons, one atop the leafy oak of Zeus and the others on either side of it on the ground. Clearly, local tradition spoke of three birds but Herodotus modified this to suit his own theory, which was that the Greeks had adopted the names of all their gods from Egypt. It is, in fact, very improbable that there was any connection between the Theban sanctuary of Zeus Ammon and Dodona. The pigeon also occurs as a symbol of the great nature-goddess – perhaps also as a manifestation of the goddess herself – on small Minoan-Mycenaean works of art.

Fine silver coins minted in the third century BC depict the divine pair and a bull within an oak-wreath. The bull was sacred to the goddess and its sacrificial slaughter was performed with a double-axe; its blood was thought to fertilize the soil. The boar, too, featured in the Dodonaean cult: Pausanias states that several new-born animals were sacrificed annually by being cast into a pit at the shrine of Demeter at Potniae in Boeotia, reappearing next year at Dodona.

The form and name of the sanctuary, the symbols of Zeus Naios, his surname itself and the priests' way of life – all these factors indicate the prior existence of an earth-cult. At Olympia and Delphi, too, Zeus and Apollo had been preceded by the prehistoric earth-goddess Gaea, from whom the sanctuary's prophetic powers were thought to derive. Pausanias (x, 12, 10) writes that the priestesses of Dodona had from time immemorial extolled the goddess Gaea as follows: 'Zeus was, Zeus is, Zeus will be. O Mighty Zeus! Earth bestows fruits; therefore call her Mother Earth.'

Worship of the oak tree had nothing to do with the Aegean tree-cult. We do not know the original significance of the oak among Indo-Europeans. It was connected with death-cults, with Hades, Poseidon and Demeter, as we can tell from certain extremely ancient Greek sanctuaries, e.g. in Arcadia and at Dodona. The tree sacred to Zeus was the small Valonia oak (*Quercus aegilops*) native to Greece. Oak trees have often been struck by lightning, a fact from which the ancients inferred the presence of the god and the sanctity of the place in question.

Three superimposed cult-layers can be distinguished at Dodona. Originally, late in the third and early in the second millennia BC, there existed the cult of the pre-Greek earth-goddess who in the Aegean area represented fertility. Her sacred creatures were the bull, boar and pigeon, and her attribute was the double-axe. When the Thesproti migrated to Epirus at the beginning of the second millennium BC they brought with them the Indo-European cult of the oak, which bore certain resemblances to the Minoan-Mycenaean tree-cult. Hence goddess and tree came to be jointly worshipped, and the tree became the goddess's venerable abode, as we can see on a number of Minoan and Mycenaean gold rings and seals.

When the Greek god Zeus won supremacy at Dodona, the ancient female deity became his consort and assumed the feminine form of his name. Her age-old cult-symbols were transferred to him and the sacred

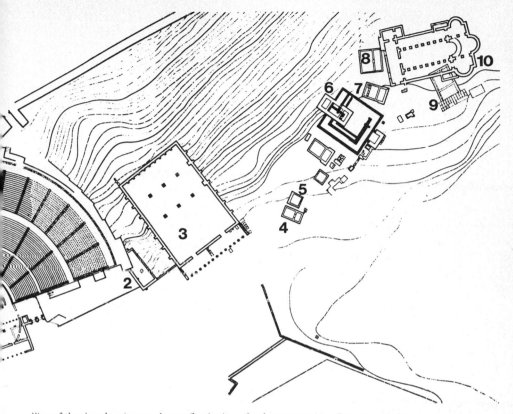

Plan of the site, showing: 1, theatre (beginning of 3rd century BC); 2, Prytaneum (4th century); Bouleuterion (3rd century); 4, temple of Aphrodite (beginning of 3rd century); 5, temple of Themis (3rd century); 6, temple of Zeus; 7, new temple of Dione; 8, old temple of Dione; 9, temple of Heracles; 10, Christian basilica. The solid black outline indicates the temple and sanctuary in the 5th-4th century.

tree became his dwelling-place. Zeus dominated Dodona for as long as the ancient cult survived. Acts of worship took place in the open until the end of the fifth century BC, the period when the first temple originated. Gradually (early in the third century BC) other temples grew up as Dodona became the home of Themis, Aphrodite, Dionysus, Apollo and Heracles.

A temple, 13 × 20 ft, was erected *c.* 400 BC beside the sacred oak, possibly to house the cult-statue of Zeus and the votive gifts presented to him. Around it were the modest huts which accommodated the Selli. During the second half of the fourth century BC a low isodomic perimeter was built to replace the tripods which had hitherto enclosed the sacred precinct. The entrance was in the south. The tutelary significance of the tripods, which no longer surrounded the sanctuary, was maintained by the erection of a contrivance dedicated by the people of Corcyra (modern Corfu). It is said to have consisted of two columns, one of which supported the small bronze statue of a boy holding a whip, the other a cauldron. Whenever the wind blew – which it usually did at Dodona – the whip struck the cauldron and made it reverberate.

The sanctuary remained very simple until the time of Alexander the Great (356–323 BC). Alexander, son of Philip II and Olympias of Epirus, planned to rebuild six Greek sanctuaries, Dodona among them. Diodorus states that the estimates for Dodona ran to fifteen hundred talents, or nine million Attic drachmae. Alexander's early death frustrated the scheme, which was ultimately put into effect by the Molossian king, Pyrrhus (297–272 BC). No changes were made in the temple itself, but the low perimeter wall was replaced by three Ionic colonnades which enclosed the inner courtyard and the sacred oak of Zeus; the east side remained open.

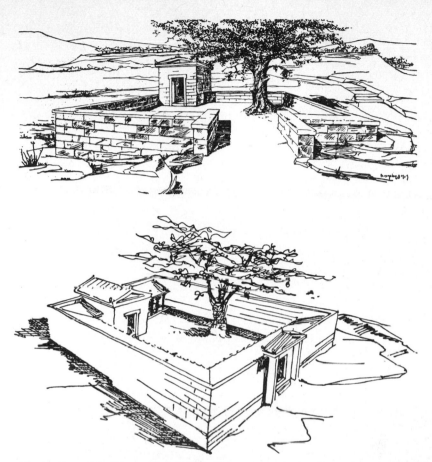

The dwelling-place of Zeus: reconstructions of the sanctuary in the 4th century BC, and after the addition of Ionic colonnades in the 3rd century.

◄ The theatre seen from the west.

Also built at the same time were the theatre, which held between eighteen and twenty thousand spectators, and the Bouleuterion, a rectangular building 106 × 130 ft, used for meeting by representatives of the Epirote tribes and the *koinon*, or Epirote community. The Prytaneum, in which priests and official guests took their meals, was renovated.

Dione was worshipped in the older temple, next to that of Zeus; Aphrodite in a temple with two octagonal columns in front; and Heracles, here regarded as the mythical ancestor of Pyrrhus, in a temple with a portico adorned with four Doric columns. Pyrrhus imported the cult of Heracles, which was linked with the mythical lineage of the Epirotes, from Eryx in western Sicily. The kings of Epirus sought to invest the oracle with new splendour and glorify their heroic ancestry.

Ancient myths, down to and including the lost epic *Nostoi* (eighth century BC), relate that the Molossi traced their descent partly from Phthia in Thessaly and partly from Troy. Phthia was regarded as the home of Achilles, and Troy as that of Andromache, Hector's widow, who was brought to Epirus in captivity by Achilles' son Neoptolemus. The latter became the mythical ancestor of Pyrrhus of Epirus. The Trojan myths enjoyed a particular revival during the reign of Pyrrhus. The Naia, a festival in honour of Zeus comprising athletic, musical and dramatic contests, was celebrated with great pomp, and the worship of

Reconstruction of the sanctuary at the end of the 3rd century BC.

deities and heroes such as Aphrodite and Heracles confirmed the ancient links with Neoptolemus, Achilles and Troy.

In 218 BC the sanctuary was overrun by marauders from neighbouring Aetolia. The historian Polybius recounts that they set the buildings ablaze, destroyed votive offerings, and demolished the 'sacred house' in which various documents were stored. A few surviving decrees were found in the temple of Zeus, which shows no evidence of burning. This suggests that the temple of Zeus and the 'sacred house' referred to by Polybius are identical. Evidently, religious awe deterred the Aetolians from setting fire to the temple of Zeus, if only to spare the sacred oak.

After 218 BC the Epirotes and Philip V of Macedon rebuilt the sanctuary with funds captured at Thermum, seat of the Aetolian Confederacy. The new temple was substantially larger, having a propylon with four Ionic columns on the façade and an adyton (inner sanctuary) behind the cella. The sacred oak was again enclosed by a colonnade in the shape of an open rectangle. The temple of Dione and the Prytaneum were abandoned, but other buildings were restored and a new and grander temple was erected for the consort of Zeus. Dodona's two principal goddesses, Dione and Themis, were somewhat overshadowed by Zeus, and their subordinate status is reflected in the layout of their temples.

The sanctuary remained unaltered until 168–167 BC, when the Romans occupied Epirus and destroyed seventy townships of varying size, Dodona included. The emperors Augustus and Hadrian gave Dodona a second lease of life. During the Augustan period the theatre was converted into an arena where men fought the bulls and wild boar which had already figured in the local cult.

The Dodonaean oracle survived until late in the fourth century AD. The cult perished when Christianity gained the upper hand, probably in consequence of a decree by the Byzantine Emperor Theodosius I, who also banned the Olympic Games in AD 393. Excavations suggest that the ancient oak of Zeus was felled and uprooted in 392.

During the fifth century a three-aisled Christian basilica was built east of the temple of Zeus. The history of Dodona was probably terminated by the invasion of the Goths (mid-sixth century AD) and by a violent earthquake which shook the whole of Greece.

S. DAKARIS

General view of the ruins of Delos, with the harbour beyond.

Delos

Legend relates that Poseidon pushed some mountains into the sea with his trident and made them take root in the sea-bed so that they could never regain the mainland, thus creating the Aegean Cyclades. The poet Callimachus states that the Nymph Asteria, when a young girl, leapt from heaven into the Aegean to escape the tempestuous wooing of Zeus, father of the gods. She became a small island floating in the sea; sailors espied her in the Gulf of Saros, again in the Straits of Euripus, and – all on the same day – near Chalcidice, off the Attic coast, and off the islands of Chios and Samos. She let herself be rocked by the deep, heedless of tide or current. Asteria's progress continued unchecked until, one day, she was moved by a pregnant woman's pleas for help; this was Leto, shortly to bear a child by Zeus and persecuted on that account by his angry consort Hera. Ignoring Hera's jealous fury, Asteria granted Leto asylum and asked in return that the child she bore should protect and honour her. Leto promised on behalf of her unborn child – Apollo – that Asteria would be granted a sanctuary of supreme splendour. Asteria remained in the midst of the Cyclades, raised above the sea-bed on four columns, and 'Zeus made her visible to all'. The island has been called Delos ever since.

Here, beneath a palm tree at the foot of Mount Cynthus, Leto gave birth to Apollo. This legend, which is recounted in the Homeric hymn to Apollo and recurs in Callimachus (*Hymn to Delos*, l. 1) and Pindar (*Prosodion*, 1), is obviously a poetic re-creation of natural phenomena that once occurred in the Aegean. It was later enlisted to explain the choice of so small and infertile an island as a pan-Hellenic place of worship and the Ionians' main religious centre in the eastern Mediterranean.

Delos is situated in the middle of the Cyclades, which may owe their name to the 'circle' (*kyklos*) formation in which they are grouped. The island is tiny – little more than three miles long and considerably less than a mile across at its widest point. Mount Cynthus, only 368 ft high, is its highest point – which may explain why the legendary mariners so often lost sight of Asteria. Its shores are rugged, inhospitable and eroded by the sea; the small harbour, a scene of bustling activity in ancient times, is still in use. Delos has little fresh water and no rivers, and the erstwhile torrent Inopus is now a marsh. Thanks to the island's sandstone-on-granite composition, however, rainwater accumulated between the two layers in natural wells and man-made cisterns which have been found in the course of excavation.

The flora consists of bushes and wild flowers. Some wild fig trees can be seen among the ruins, also a few plots of melons cultivated by people from Mykonos. Ancient inscriptions testify, however, that vines, olives and figs used to flourish on the estate of the Apollonian sanctuary, and archaeologists have found numerous leases concluded between the priesthood and peasantry. Other inscriptions show that there were gardens near the shrine of Leto, a grove in the sacred precinct, and estates which bore the names 'Phoenix', 'Palm' and 'Laurel'.

Delos has probably been inhabited since the third millennium BC. Its initial function was that of a refuge and base for seafarers undertaking the long and hazardous voyage from Asia Minor to the Greek mainland. It was later settled by a few fishermen-pirates. According to Thucydides, the first settlement was established by Carians from Asia Minor; Mount Cynthus has yielded the remains of a dozen or so huts.

The other Aegean islands, far more fertile and richer in mineral resources, developed a brisk trade with the coast of Asia Minor and mainland Greece, whereas excavations on Delos indicate that its own period of prosperity did not occur until early in the fourteenth century BC. The inhabitants became more numerous and moved from Mount Cynthus to a coastal site which later became that of the Apollonian sanctuary. The earlier sanctuaries whose remains have been excavated there betray no obvious association with any particular deity, and probably served the cult of some Mycenaean goddess. These earlier buildings form a single unit and can now be seen to the west of the oldest temple of Apollo. Their ground-plan recalls palaces of the Minoan and Mycenaean periods, though the characteristic megaron (central room with hearth) is lacking.

166

When did Apollo come to Delos? Neither ancient sources nor modern excavations have made it possible to identify the time and place of his arrival beyond doubt. It is assumed that the cult of Apollo was imported into Delos by Ionian seafarers at about the turn of the first millennium BC, the period when the Ionians were asserting their mastery over the Mediterranean. Their young tutelary god, who was already worshipped at the sanctuaries of Claros and Didyma in Asia Minor, came to Delos as a newborn child, the son and brother of two oriental goddesses – Lycian Leto and Lydian Artemis – who were successors of the pre-Hellenic fertility-goddess formerly worshipped throughout the Aegean. The legendary persecution of oriental Leto by 'jealous' Greek Hera may reflect the fact that it was only with difficulty that gods from the East secured a foothold in Greek religious life.

Apollo never entirely lost his Asiatic traits on Delos, a fact which encouraged his rapid identification with pre-Hellenic deities and a ready acceptance of the numerous oriental cults to which Delos was exposed in Hellenistic and Roman times. Delian Apollo assumed the function and characteristics of his pre-Hellenic antecedents, was only later adopted by the Greeks, and moved – probably during the eighth century BC – from Delos into the pantheon of the Olympian gods. He developed into one of the major deities and was destined in the fullness of time to become an expression of the Greek ethos at its most consummate. He was the only Greek god permitted to retain his name during the Roman Imperial era.

Apart from Apollo's arrival, the eighth century witnessed an upturn in the fortunes of the island which had harnessed its destiny to his. Once a modest haven for sailors, it became a religious centre and a commercial and maritime power. The prestige which Delos enjoyed for centuries began to wane only when Apollo was displaced by other deities.

Ancient sources describe the splendid festivals held annually at Delos to celebrate Apollo's birth. These religious festivals and games were attended by Ionians from all over the Aegean and the western coasts of Asia Minor (*Hymn to Delian Apollo*, l. 147; and Thucydides (III, 104, 4–6). The Delia were evidently promoted by Athens, just as it was Athens which cultivated the Delian sanctuary's renown from Archaic times until the Christian era. From the reign of the sixth-century tyrant Pisistratus onwards, the Athenians linked their own ancient legends concerning Delos wth the Apollonian sanctuary there, e.g. the myth of the Hyperborean maidens who voyaged to Delos and, above all, the legend of Theseus. His return from Crete to Athens was regarded as the basis of Athenian claims to political control over the sanctuary at Delos, for it was there that Theseus gave thanks to Apollo for his own and his companions' deliverance from the Minotaur. They made sacrifice to the god, presented him with a statue of Aphrodite which had been entrusted to them by Ariadne, and performed a dance whose monotonous and serpentine (meandering) steps commemorated their wanderings in the Labyrinth. Theseus performed this dance (known as the *geranos* or crane-dance) round the altar, the Keraton, made by Apollo from the horns of goats slain by his sister Artemis. Plutarch (*Theseus*, 21) describes this dance, as does the poet Callimachus (*Hymn to Delos*, l. 307). Many details remain obscure, however, notably a strange custom observed by Aegean sailors and merchants. After landing at Delos, they used to run round the altar, thrashing either it or each other and biting the trunk of the sacred olive tree.

Theseus is also credited with having founded the first games and presented a palm frond to the victor. In 425 BC the Delia were reorganized, and were henceforward held every four years in conjunction with musical performances attended by an Attic delegation of one hundred members, who sailed to Delos in a ship built specially for the occasion.

The Athenian dominion over Delos was marked by the first *katharsis* (purification), decreed by Pisistratus in obedience to an oracular pronouncement of ancient date. It was forbidden to bury the dead on the island because Apollo abominated death. *Katharsis* at that time applied only to the sanctuary and not to the entire island (Thucydides, III, 104).

Athenian control of Delos really began in the fifth century BC, when the Athenians took over the administration of temple funds and removed the Delian treasury to Athens. Having gained a foothold in Delos, Athens used the cult of Apollo to help it acquire and retain maritime control of the Aegean – a striking example of interdependence between religion and political supremacy.

With the second *katharsis* of 426 BC, the Athenians reinforced their position in Delos. This time, according to Thucydides, they removed all

The remains of the colossal Archaic statue of Apollo.

existing graves and transferred them to the neighbouring island of Rheneia. The finds made on Rheneia are now in Mykonos Museum. Henceforward, no one was permitted to die or give birth on Delos, and inscriptions detail the measures to be taken in the event of drowned men being washed up on the Delian coast. Only the very ancient mythical graves were left *in situ*.

In 422 BC, presumably for political reasons which have never been ascertained, the Athenians supplemented *katharsis* by evacuating the island's entire population. After the Delians had spent a considerable time in Asia Minor and many had perished in massacres, the Athenians annulled their harsh decree and permitted the survivors to return 'by order of the Delphic god'.

View across the sacred precinct of the temple of Apollo.

◄ The House of the Dolphins: general view of the interior (below), and detail of mosaic floor.

Visitors to the ruined town of Delos will see the remains of handsome buildings and the mosaics in their courtyards. These mosaics, left *in situ* after excavation, display geometric and polychrome designs, e.g. dolphins, tridents, masks, and representations of Dionysus riding a panther or tiger.

On the north-west side of the island, beside the ancient harbour, lie the sacred precinct of Apollo and the public buildings that surround it. The buildings date from such a variety of periods that the general impression is one of extreme confusion. The first of these is the 'House of the Naxians', erected in 560 BC and deriving its name from a votive offering from the island of Naxos, a colossal statue of a youth, which was found beside it.

The Sacred Way which leads to the three temples of Apollo is flanked by bases that once supported votive gifts. The material of the north temple is limestone; only the foundations of the *prodomos* (vestibule) and cella survive. In its workmanship, this building resembles temples on the Acropolis at Athens dating from the time of Pisistratus. The central 'Temple of the Athenians' or 'Temple of the Seven Statues' was begun after the *katharsis* of 426 BC and consecrated in 417. The third in the series is the 'Great Temple', the only peripteral building on the island, twice begun and never completed. Its structural phases are dated 475 and post-314, in parallel with Delian history. Building began when Delos was the centre of a cultural association, was discontinued when the Athenians transferred the Delian treasury to their own city, and was resumed after Delos had freed itself from Attic sovereignty. None of the temples was intended to replace another and all were built independently and successively. Another interesting point is that the Delian temples of Apollo were the least pretentious of all the shrines erected in his honour, temples elsewhere being of great splendour.

To the east stood the fifth-century Prytaneum, where the *prytaneis* (presiding officers) met and feasted; this building also housed the sanctuary's archives. The ground-plan is symmetrically divided into two parts, containing the spacious hall and vestibule mentioned in inscriptions. Beyond the Prytaneum is a very singular and mysterious building, the celebrated 'Monument of the Bulls'. Its function remains obscure, but its strangely elongated shape has given rise to numerous conjectures. The most likely theory is that it housed a ship which the Macedonian king Demetrius Poliorcetes presented to Apollo in gratitude for a naval victory. The monument derives its name from the bulls which supported its capitals. In the north lies the Stoa (portico) of Antigonus, son of Demetrius Poliorcetes, which dates from the third century BC. This too features ornamental bulls.

Forward of the Stoa stood the celebrated 'Theke', also mentioned by Herodotus (IV, 35). Mycenaean potsherds were found here. The Theke was traditionally held to be the tomb of the Hyperborean maidens, Opis and Argis, who came from the north to assist Leto in childbirth. This legend, too, stresses Apollo's links with the north, for it was to the land of the Hyperboreans that he customarily withdrew in winter. A similar

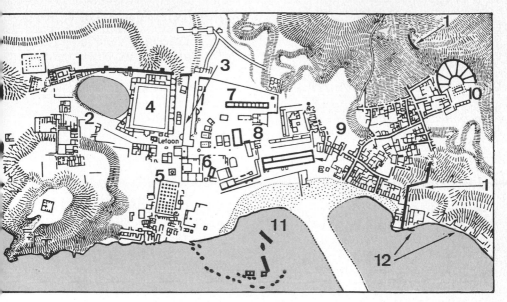

Plan of the sacred precinct: 1, wall of Triarias; 2, lake; 3, hall of Antigonus; 4, market place; 5, hall of columns; 6, sanctuary of Artemis; 7, hall of the bulls; 8, temple of Apollo; 9, hall of Philip V; 10, theatre; 11, harbour; 12, quays.

construction may be placed on the 'Sema', the tomb of two other Hyperborean maidens named Laodice and Hyperoche, which is situated on the way from the limestone temple to the sanctuary's western boundary. Further east lies the most sacred altar, the Keraton, where Theseus made sacrifice and the crane-dance was performed.

The Artemision, situated west of the temple of Apollo, was dedicated to the god's twin sister. It is the oldest Delian sanctuary, whose origins go back to the second millenium BC. Rich Mycenaean votive offerings were found here. Its proximity to the tombs of the Hyperborean maidens is yet another pointer to the sanctuary's great age, to its links with pre-Hellenic deities and tree-worship. Literary sources state that the Artemision was originally the enclosed area in which the sacred tree grew. The Ephesian temple of Artemis in Asia Minor provides further indications of the links between Artemis and tree-worship. What is more, traces have been found in Delos of the Mycenaean enclosure

173

View from the temple of Isis towards the harbour.

One of the lions lining the ceremonial avenue dedicated by the Naxians. ▶

surrounding the sacred precinct, which was about 50 ft long. The
Mycenaean sanctuary of Artemis was replaced in the seventh century BC
by the Archaic temple, which was in turn absorbed – in a good state of
preservation – by the Hellenistic building.

North of it, in the Lake Quarter, we come to the temple of the Twelve
Olympian Gods (Dodekatheon), also to the temple of Leto (Letoön) and
the renowned Avenue of the Lions, which was probably a votive gift

from the island of Naxos. This masterpiece of Archaic art, the only sculptural parade of wild beasts in all Greece, drew its inspiration from the East; the lions guarded the route to the sanctuary of Leto.

Reaching the granite Palaestra, we come to the edge of this quarter. North-east of it, in the Stadium Quarter, stood the Archigesion, or sanctuary of the Delians' mythical ancestor Anius, a son of Apollo whom only native islanders were permitted to worship. A rectangular synagogue erected in the first century BC used to stand near by.

We must not overlook the group of buildings between the temples of Apollo and the propylaea. This includes the Aphrodision, a marble temple of Aphrodite dating from the fourth century BC, and, in the River Inopus Quarter, the Terrace of the Foreign Gods, with the Serapeion (temple of Isis), the Samothrakeion, the monument of Mithridates, the sanctuary of the Syrian gods and the Greek temple of Hera. This quarter also boasted some spacious and well-constructed buildings such as the House of Hermes, of which three ruined storeys survive.

Steps ascend Mount Cynthus in the south. At its summit we find the island's earliest place of worship, together with the remains of some prehistoric huts. Near by is the *antron*, a cave which in Hellenistic times contained a sanctuary of the hero Heracles.

Delos is permanently associated with Apollo, a blithe and cheerful god who took possession of the island by right of birth, not with the violence that attended his accession at Delphi, a god who hated death and was celebrated with songs and dances. The mildness of Delian Apollo's 'image' may be attributable to its creation by peaceful, open-hearted islanders dwelling in a world of radiant Mediterranean light. The priests of Delian Apollo conformed to this image and had little in common with the stern and exacting priesthood of Delphi. They administered their god's finances shrewdly and skilfully. The bustling commercial centre owed its prosperity to Apollo. Leto had kept the pledge she made to Asteria.

VANNA HADJIMIHALI

◄ The three-storey House of Hermes.

Reconstruction of the stoa (see p. 184).

Samos : the Heraeum

The capital of the Aegean island of Samos once stood on its northern coast, facing the near-by promontory of Mycale in Asia Minor. The site of the ancient city is now occupied by the small township of Tigani, lately renamed Pythagoreion. Nearly four miles to the west, on the edge of the plain of Chora, lay the sanctuary of Hera, the island's goddess. A single column rising from the ruins near the sea is all that marks the spot today, near the mouth of the river Imbrasus. Having no impressive ruins to show, the Heraeum preserves the fascination peculiar to ancient, hallowed soil. Thanks to the island's wealth of archaeological finds, religious traditions and historical fact, however, we can trace the development of this ancient centre of worship with unusual continuity. Archaeological discoveries serve chiefly to illuminate this continuity. Credit for the exemplary way in which excavations have been conducted must go to that great teacher of archaeology, Ernst Buschor, whose name will always be associated with the Heraeum of Samos.

During the latter half of the third millenium BC a small village community grew up between the rivers Imbrasus and Chisius, enclosed by a protective wall. The people of the Early and Middle Bronze Age worshipped a deity of the earth and of fertility. Their village settlement was destroyed as a result of earthquake, fire or war. Early in the Mycenaean period, or *c.* 1500 BC, new migrants – possibly the first to speak Greek – built a larger settlement and surrounded it with a stout rampart. Their place of worship was inside this rampart. Excavation revealed a paved floor at whose centre stood the lygos or chaste tree (*Vitex agnus castus*). Its stump and roots, submerged in ground-water for many centuries, came to light in 1963. The nature-goddess who manifested herself in this tree, and to whom devotees made sacrifice on a neighbouring stone altar, was Hera's predecessor. Even when this settlement, too, was destroyed at the end of the Mycenaean period, those who had escaped destruction continued to pray round the lygos tree and altar. Tradition and modern research agree that *c.* 1050 BC a new wave of settlers migrated to Samos, this time from Argos. They brought with them the cult of the great Argive goddess Hera, which became amalgamated with the ancient local cult, and found that the lygos sacred to Hera in Argos also grew abundantly in their new home.

Samian cult-legend claimed that Hera was born beneath the lygos tree itself. Having spent her childhood and youth there, she later wedded Zeus at the spot where, according to tradition, the inhabitants discovered the 'image of the goddess', a rough-hewn 'board of singular shape' not made by human hand. The pre-Greek cult was transferred to the Hera of Samos, thus uniting the worship of deities from two different worlds. Thereafter, the Heraeum developed in the manner of most Greek sanctuaries and reflected the various phases of its cult, also of the architecture and sculpture engendered by it.

The boundaries of the sacred precinct were marked by an outer enclosure or by boundary-stones bearing inscriptions. Worship, whose essential precondition was the god's presence, took place within these boundaries, within which the divine presence might be manifested in a tree, spring or rock. The Heraeum's earliest altar consisted of natural limestone and was built facing the spring of the dog-star Sirius; there was clearly a connection between the star's appearance in the sky and the festivals of Hera. During sacrifice the goddess's cult-statue was placed on a stone plinth near the lygos tree, and afterwards it was returned to a small chapel which stood behind the plinth. East of the altar a road ran down to the sea, where the goddess's effigy received the purificatory bath which annually restored her youth and virginity.

Until the tenth century BC tree, altar, plinth, idol and chapel constituted the original Heraeum where worshippers paid homage to the consort of the paramount Olympian god in all her roles: as patroness of marriage, fertility and increase – in short, as goddess of womankind. Here Aphrodite, who had taken on functions similar to those of Hera, assumed an ancillary role.

The 'venerable board' remained the Heraeum's cult-idol until the end of antiquity. Animals were sacrificed and other offerings presented to this baulk of timber, which was annually dressed in opulent robes donated by the faithful. An inscription lists various garments woven in the sanctuary itself by women from the city. Even when a second effigy in human shape was produced for the cult of Hera, both idols continued to exist side by side. In the eyes of her devotees, precedence still went to the piece of wood that had been hallowed by tradition.

The *hieros gamos*, or sacred wedding of Hera to Zeus, took place every spring and was the major event of the year. In Archaic times, the procession included warriors in armour. Hera was fêted as a virgin, bride and spouse. Few details of this mystic festival are known, but similar festivals such as the sacred marriage of Hera and Zeus at Knossos and Argos and the singular cult in Boeotia, the Daedala, indicate that these acts of worship were associated with primordial generation, in other words, the union of male and female in the context of creation. The cult of Hera is illustrated by a small wood-carving which shows the divine pair standing together, Zeus embracing Hera.

Another festival of Hera was the so-called 'Rope Festival' (Toneia), held at the end of July when the lygos trees were covered in bluish or whitish blossom and pilgrims flocked to the sanctuary. It was part of the ritual that the cult-idol should be lifted from its plinth and carried down to the shore. After being purified in the sea it was dressed in new robes, offered cakes and bound with ropes to a lygos tree.

Legends exist to explain most acts of worship. One Samian saga tells how Tyrrhenian pirates tried to carry off the cult-idol but found, when they took it aboard, that they were unable to put to sea. They carried it ashore again, placed some sacrificial cakes (*psaista*) in front of it, and sailed off as fast as they could. The Samians searched desperately for their cult-idol and eventually discovered it hidden beneath a lygos tree. Believing that it had walked to the sea unaided, they used some lygos twigs to bind it to the trunk against which the pirates had propped it.

Similar legends still survive in various parts of Greece: Keffalinia and Naxos, for example, have a story that pirates once stole the icon of the Virgin from a monastery. They, too, found it impossible to set sail despite a favourable wind, and the spell was not lifted until they had cast the icon overboard.

Another Samian act of worship was the washing of the divine robes, which took place from the seventh century BC onwards, probably in a cistern beside the river Imbrasus, less than a hundred yards south of the temple.

The sacrificial cakes associated with the idol's miraculous deliverance from pirates are said to have been a Samian 'speciality'. The other votive and sacrificial offerings – fruit, wine, honey, oil and milk – were pan-Hellenic in character. During animal sacrifices, the portions of the beast reserved for the goddess were burnt on the altar. Other cuts were roasted and distributed among the faithful, whose shared repast was thought to ensure communion with the goddess. Archaeological finds suggest that fragrant woods and herbs were burnt in Hera's honour. One typical discovery was a small bronze vessel used for burnt offerings. The Heraeum yielded a particularly impressive *kernos,* a peculiar cult-vessel surrounded by smaller ones. These vessels took the form of male and female heads and were found close to others in the shape of a bull's and lion's head, a frog, a monkey and a pomegranate. Another discovery was the wooden statuette of a kneeling boy which may once have adorned a lyre, which would prove that instrumental music played as important a role in the worship of Hera as it did in other Greek cults. It has also been inferred from the discovery of grotesque clay masks that dances and even a kind of mime play were performed – a common feature of divine worship throughout the ancient world.

Responsibility for the Heraeum and the performance of rites was entrusted to the Priestess of Hera, probably commemorating the fact that Hera's first priestess, Admete, was driven from Argos and reputedly brought the cult of Hera to the island. There were also priests, public administrators, guards, vendors, workmen and numerous auxiliary staff.

The requirements of the Hera cult, coupled with the need to construct places of worship for Aphrodite and Hermes, led to increased building activity.

One milestone in the Heraeum's history was the erection of the first large temple in 800 BC. This *hekatompedos naos,* or hundred-foot temple, was the sanctuary's earliest monumental structure. Measuring 108 × 21 ft, it had a pitched roof, and the timber at its apex was supported by thirteen or fourteen wooden columns running down its long axis. Inside, in front

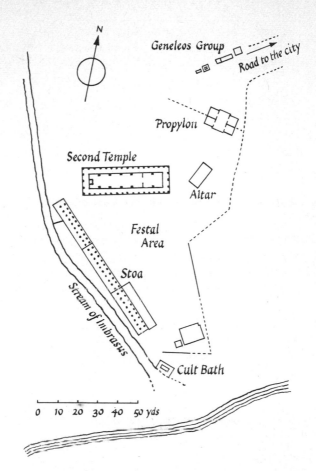

Plan of the Heraeum site.

of the (west) rear wall the cult-idol reposed on a stone base, which has survived.

After the altar had been renovated yet again, the paved floor on which it stood was extended to include the lygos tree. Numerous bronze votive gifts of this period permit us to conclude that the islanders had an advanced bronze-founding technique. The turn of the eighth–seventh centuries brought with it an architectural innovation as radical as the building of the very first temple: annexed to the old 'hundred-foot temple' was a peristasis or ambulatory of 7 × 17 wooden columns. This signalled the genesis of the peripteral type of temple.

183

In the century that followed, the Heraeum underwent various architectural changes which render this period important – if not supremely important – in the history of art. Hellas gave birth to monumental sculpture. There also came into being the first temple conceived as a peripteros and executed as such – i.e. unlike the earlier structures, it did not have a colonnade added subsequently. This new temple, erected on the foundations of the old, had a spacious cella. In place of the former row of columns, wooden beams now reinforced the side walls which supported the enlarged roof. The base of the cult-idol was located on the central axis so that visitors found themselves facing Hera's effigy when they entered the temple. The walls were for the first time built entirely of stone and culminated in a frieze portraying devotees in procession at the festival of Hera. The roof timbers were covered with clay tiles. Wooden columns on stone plinths – a double row on the east side – foreshadowed the later monumental temples of Ionia. (The temple's wooden members were probably adorned with bronze, and the transverse beams above the columns with bronze volutes, precursors of the Ionic capital.) At this period too Hera acquired her cult-statue in human shape. Its probable attribution to the Aeginetan sculptor Smilis means that, even at this early date, leading artists were active outside their native cities.

The first Greek stoa, a 230-ft covered walk with a double colonnade, was erected beside the temple to shield pilgrims from the sun and rain. South of the stoa was the carefully constructed cistern in which, among other ritual acts, the washing of the goddess's robes took place.

Late in the sixth century BC some smaller buildings were erected near the altar, probably temples of Aphrodite and Hermes, also treasure-chambers for the safekeeping of valuable votive gifts. Life-size and over-life-size statues of gods and men, beasts and spirits, flanked the roads of the Heraeum, notably the processional routes. A series of plinths have been discovered: one such base consisted of nine juxtaposed members and may have supported an entire ship – possibly that of Colaeus, who was driven as far as the Pillars of Heracles (Gibraltar) in 638 BC, negotiated the straits and landed at Tartessus on the Atlantic coast of Spain. Herodotus (IV, 52) writes of a huge bronze vessel supported by three over-life-size figures which the valiant sea-captain dedicated to

Hera on returning from his epic voyage. Hundreds of bronze griffins' heads of the sort which adorned the rim of this vessel have been dug up and can now be seen in Vathi Museum on Samos.

The Heraeum attained its prime half-way through the sixth century BC, when Samos rose to become one of the strongest maritime powers of its day. Work began *c.* 570 BC on an ambitious project directed by the Samian architects Rhoecus and Theodorus: the construction of a vast new temple, which was destined to be destroyed soon after its completion. Theodorus seems to have been an uncommonly versatile artist. An architect, bronze-founder, sculptor and goldsmith, he had already collaborated on the Artemisium at Ephesus and the Scias in Sparta. He is also reputed to have invented the technique of hollow casting and wrote a treatise on the temple of Samos. As a very old man he produced the legendary ring of Polycrates.

Before building began, the old buildings were demolished and the waters of the Imbrasus diverted to make room for the new temple, which measured 176 × 354 ft and was the first Ionic dipteros, with a double colonnade along the sides and a triple one at either end. It may have been this maze-like profusion of columns – 104 fluted ones in the outer series and 30 inside them – which prompted the ancients to refer to the building as the 'Labyrinth'.

The altar still faced in the same direction, even though it had been seven times modified and rebuilt. In the days of Rhoecus and Theodorus a new altar was erected in fine brown (Poros) limestone, parallel with the temple frontage. Lygos tree and altar were enclosed by walls in the form of an open rectangle. Reliefs adorned the top and inner face of the walls. As in the case of most Greek temples, bronze statues were the first objects to be looted in later years. Only some small votive offerings in bronze have survived to convey an idea of the beauty of their larger companions, now lost. The surviving sculptures in marble provide more eloquent testimony. Fragments of an over-life-size statue of a naked youth (*kouros*) and that of a worshipper leading his calf to the goddess's sacrificial altar combine to illustrate the notable Samian contribution to pan-Hellenic portrayals of the male nude.

Female figures, their slender limbs fetchingly clad in Ionian *chiton* and *himation,* their heads and shoulders sometimes draped in veils, provide what is perhaps the most cogent evidence of the high standard attained by Samian artists. Of the two handsome statues dedicated to the goddess by a certain Cheramys, one is in the Louvre and the other in Berlin. We do not know the sculptor's name, though the name of one of his contemporaries – presumably a pupil – has survived. A group of figures consisting of two women, one seated and one standing, and a reclining man (in Vathi Museum) bears the inscription 'Geneleos made us'.

Long rows of votive statues flanked the roads of the sanctuary and thronged its open places. Votive gifts in marble and clay proclaimed the wealth of men and their faith in the great Samian goddess whose fame had spread to the most sequestered corners of the Greek world.

Halfway through the sixth century Samos was ushered into a golden age by the tyrant Polycrates. Religion, art and the island's economy all received a powerful fillip. About 530 BC the Samians embarked on a temple of Hera which was to surpass all its predecessors in size and splendour. Measuring 180 × 365 ft, it was a dipteros with 123 columns.

A fallen column-drum at the temple of Hera built by Polycrates.

Statue group by Geneleos. Vathi Museum.

The vast project was only begun during Polycrates' lifetime and, like the temple of Zeus at Olympia, it remained under construction for generations, until the beginning of the third century BC. Even so, the roof of the cella was never more than a temporary one.

Polycrates maintained an entourage of outstanding figures: among those who invested his court with renown and prestige were the poets Anacreon and Ibycus, Pythagoras' father Mnesarchus (famed on account of his seals), the ageing Rhoecus and Theodorus, and the prominent architect Eupalinus.

Eupalinus of Megara cut through Mount Ampelus – starting from either end he drove a thousand-yard tunnel through the rock to carry the city's water-supply. Herodotus refers to Eupalinus' conduit, the mole at Samos and the Samian temple of Hera as the Greeks' three mightiest feats of engineering. Polycrates' temple, 'the largest known', rated as one of the seven wonders of the world even though it was never completed. It was sited 130 ft west of its predecessor, possibly in order to create a larger festival site round the altar. The plinth of Hera's cult-statue, which had been built over but not destroyed by Rhoecus' temple, came to light during construction. This venerable relic was now given a setting worthy of its status in the shape of a pavilion with wooden columns. The cult-idols of Hera were housed in the temple of Aphrodite while building was in progress. The same period witnessed the consecration of a joint temple to Hermes and Aphrodite and a large Ionic temple to the sibling deities Apollo and Artemis. The spacious vestibule of the latter building has prompted archaeologists to conclude that it was also an odeum (small theatre).

Polycrates' violent death did not interrupt work in progress but inhibited the Heraeum's development. A large number of bronze statuettes, among them a work by the Athenian sculptor Myron portraying Athena flanked by Zeus and Heracles, were erected, but the Golden Age of the Heraeum had passed. When, in Hellenistic times, Samos once more attained a peak of artistic activity, a final attempt was made to complete the temple of Hera. Roman incursions, piratical raids, wars and fraternal strife all left their sad mark on the Heraeum. A few small temples were built in the course of the Imperial Roman era, but the ancient faith had lost a growing measure of its power and influence.

The conduit for the city's water supply, cut by Eupalinus of Megara.

Hera's temple became an art gallery and effigies of Roman emperors invaded her divine abode. The boundaries between sacred precinct and profane land were obliterated.

The Heraeum did not escape the wholesale destruction that attended the barbarian raids of the third century A D, and tasteless essays in restoration only emphasized its decline. In the fifth century A D, the first Christian basilica arose on the ancient temple ruins. Stones that had once been consecrated to an ancient faith were reunited to form the place of Christian worship.

MANOLIS ANDRONIKOS

Head of an initiate, from a clay figure of the Hellenistic period, now in the Samothrace Museum.

Samothrace : the Sanctuary of the 'Great Gods'

Samothrace is a strange and extremely atmospheric island. Still unspoilt, it rejoices in wild and luxuriant vegetation which thrives on the water from numerous springs. The island is dominated by Mount Phengari, 5,400 ft high and snow-covered for much of the winter; wild goats frisk among its colourful crags. Fields are few because there is little level ground, and agricultural produce has always been scarce. It was the island's position which made it so important to the ancients. Situated in the windswept north-east corner of the Aegean, an area noted for its turbulent seas, it provided a haven for little ships threatened by storms; its small coves spelt safety to settlers, traders and travellers of every description.

The rugged mountain scenery inspired the early Greeks with awe of the implacable forces of nature and undoubtedly played a major part in shaping the mysterious cult which took root here. The cult of Samothrace originated prior to its occupation by Greeks, but the Greek element in which the ancient cult became absorbed had a decisive and undisputed influence on its development.

Excavations started in the last century by an Austrian team were pursued from 1938 onwards under the supervision of Karl Lehmann and, when he died, by his widow Phyllis. Further research has recently been undertaken by the American School of Classical Studies in Athens. The whole of the celebrated sanctuary of the 'Great Gods' has been excavated. This was situated on the island's north-west coast, south of Palaeopolis, an ancient town founded c. 700 BC by the earliest Greek settlers to reach the island.

As with all mystic cults in Greek antiquity, the essential core of the Mysteries remains an enigma. We are acquainted with a few minor details which recall other cults, we glean a certain amount of information from ancient writers, and we have various archaeological finds. Taking all these in conjunction, we can form a general picture of the Samothracian cult, but only a superficial one.

The island was inhabited by unknown tribes during the latter part of the Neolithic period. About 1000 BC, during the Iron Age, tribes migrated from the neighbouring coast of Thrace, mingled with the original inhabitants, and created the island's cult. It is indicative that the gods of the Samothracian Mysteries bore pre-Greek names which were adopted by the Greek settlers who migrated to the island c. 700 BC from ancient Aeolis on the coast of Asia Minor. The Greeks introduced the worship of Athena, who became tutelary goddess of the city-state founded by them.

Reverence for the forces of nature ultimately engendered a special cult, the central figure of which was the 'Great Goddess', mistress of forest and mountain, depicted on local Hellenistic coins seated between two lions. Her pre-Hellenic name was Axierus, and her characteristics resembled those of the great female deity worshipped in ancient times throughout Anatolia, also those of Phrygian Cybele and other goddesses. In the minds of the Greek settlers, she became identified with the Demeter of Greek mythology, goddess of the earth and fertility, but her pre-Hellenic name, like the names of the other 'Great Gods', survived until the end of antiquity. Archaeological finds make it clear that, in general, the island's cult bore the linguistic imprint of its pre-Hellenic inhabitants. The goddess's power was thought to have found embodiment in the island's rocks and in the iron-ore which abounded there. The stone altars in the sanctuary display gleaming veins of various colours. It was believed that the goddess granted her protection to devotees who wore iron rings made of the local metal, a form of amulet which they obtained from her sanctuary. Axierus had a cult-partner named Cadmilus, who personified fertility and was a youthful deity equated by the Greeks with Hermes; his attributes were the ram's head and herald's staff.

Worshipped in association with this pair of deities were the Cabiri, two young fertility-gods whom the Greeks identified with the Dioscuri and whose attributes were stars and a serpent. Some scholars have opined that the Cabiri were popularly identified with the brothers Dardanus and Aëtion (or Iasion), regarded in Greek mythology as founders of the Samothracian Mysteries. The Cabiri became tutelary gods of the seafarer, and the Samothracian sanctuary was filled with votive gifts that had been presented to them. The 'Great Gods' included two more deities known in the island's pre-Hellenic language as 'Axiocersus' and 'Axiocersa'. These were, in fact, the god of the underworld and his consort: Hades and Persephone.

Ancient writers were themselves presented with numerous problems of interpretation by this group of gods and their worship, with the result that we possess many conflicting accounts of their characteristics. The fact that they were worshipped in a number of other places, e.g. Lemnos, Tenedos, and Boeotia, where the Cabiri differed in age and character, only aggravated the confusion that prevailed among ancient and modern interpreters. What is certain is that the pre-Hellenic cult was adopted and assimilated by the Greeks who settled in Samothrace. It may have been due to Greek influence that the 'Great Gods' were augmented by Hades and Persephone on the pattern of the Eleusinian Mysteries (see p. 76), with which those of Samothrace had much in common.

The purpose of initiation is not hard to grasp. Candidates aspired to happiness in earthly life and tranquillity in the underworld. Like the Eleusinian Mysteries, the cult of Samothrace had two degrees of initiation, *myesis* (initiation) and *epopteia* (inspection). Anyone could be initiated in Samothrace, citizen or slave, man or woman, Greek or foreigner, young or old. Initiation took place whenever the believer desired it, not at any predetermined time. In contrast to Eleusinian convention, there was no stipulated interval between the first and second degrees of initiation, so it was possible for a candidate to receive both degrees within the space of a single day. Initiation into the second degree was not essential, though it did entail certain qualifications the nature of which remains obscure, except that a special measure of moral purity was demanded which expressed itself in some form of penance or atonement for earlier sins.

As at Eleusis, festivities took place at night, each initiate carrying a clay lamp of his own. Archaeological finds have confirmed that such lamps were generally, if not invariably, decorated with a reference to the 'Great Gods'. During initiation into the first degree, devotees were presented with a large cloth which, if worn round the hips, was thought

to offer protection from the perils of the deep. At one of the ceremonies, devotees received the iron rings which they henceforth wore as amulets. The cult of the 'Great Gods' was already established when the first Greek settlers arrived in Samothrace. A Cyclopean wall, part of which rises in front of the Anaktoron (palace), originated in the days of the pre-Hellenic inhabitants. From the sixth century BC, when the sanctuary passed into Greek custody and its festivals became more lavish, special buildings were erected for cult purposes.

Initiation into the first degree took place in the Anaktoron, part of which contained an enclosed chamber, the so-called *hiera oikia* or sacred abode. Here, prior to initiation, candidates dressed themselves in a chiton, probably white; this done, they entered the Anaktoron proper, where the rite was performed in public. When it was over they entered a chamber at the north end of the building, where the hierophant, a priest specially appointed for the purpose, showed them certain symbols whose nature has not been discovered.

Also built in the sixth century BC, at the same time as the Anaktoron, was the large 'Hall of Votive Gifts' in which all manner of votive offerings were preserved. Many of these were official presentations of great splendour, but there were also humble offerings from common people who wished to thank the 'Great Gods' for saving them from shipwreck.

Another contemporary building was the one replaced by the present sanctuary, a bow-shaped structure used for initiation into the second degree. The same period must also have witnessed the construction of yet another building situated in the centre of the sanctuary and known as the Temenos. Provided with an Ionic monumental entrance on the north side, it was the scene of ritual dances with musical accompaniment, also of the 'sacred drama' which formed part of the annual festivities.

Many of the ancient temple buildings acquired a monumental appearance during the fourth century BC. Most of them became larger and

◄ General view of the sanctuary of the 'Great Gods'; the columns still standing belong to the Anaktoron (Hall of Votive Gifts), in which Mysteries took place.

more splendid, and the Arsinoëum was added. In this, the largest circular building on Greek soil, quarters were provided for city delegations attending the sanctuary's festivities. The Propylaea were built in the third century BC, as was the monumental fountain beside which stood the celebrated 'Winged Victory' of Samothrace (now in the Louvre). A (possibly two-storeyed) stoa for visitors to the sanctuary was constructed on the south side of the site; this covered walk formed the extreme boundary of the precinct behind the theatre, which faced the monumental altar.

It is assumed that the sanctuary's annual festival took place in July, the month in which – possibly by coincidence – modern islanders celebrate their own popular and church festival in honour of St Paraskevi. Visitors flocked to the place, among them official envoys from the Greek city-states. Initiates wore garlands in their hair. There were successive sacrifices on the various altars, processions, prayers and invocations of the 'Great Gods', also other festivities of which we know very little. These appear to have included a 'sacred drama' which re-enacted the abduction of the goddess of fertility by the god of the underworld. The wedding of Cadmus and Aphrodite's daughter Harmonia formed the theme of yet another presentation. A poet from Carian Iasus won high honours for having written a tragedy entitled *Dardanus*. The huge size of the theatre proves that dramatic performances acquired major importance in the course of time.

The sanctuary earned a great reputation during the Hellenistic period. At the end of the fourth century BC the Diadochi, successors of Alexander the Great, held it in particular esteem, doubtless because it was the place where Philip II of Macedon had met and fallen in love with the Epirote princess Olympias when both were visiting Samothrace for initiation into the Mysteries; Olympias became his wife, and was the mother of Alexander the Great.

Samothrace retained its importance as a naval base throughout the turbulent period during which the Diadochi fought each other for

The Winged Victory of Samothrace, one of the best-known sculptures of antiquity, 2nd century BC. Louvre, Paris. ▶

supremacy. Such was the prestige of its sanctuary that the 'sacred island' gradually and inevitably became an asylum for political refugees. Even Perseus, the last and luckless king of Macedon, 179–168 BC, tried to escape there after his defeat by the Romans. The Romans later revered the sanctuary because of the connection between Dardanus (who was of the same stock as Aeneas, founder of Rome) and the Samothracian cult. Samothrace continued until St Paul's day to be a port of call for travellers to Greece from the coast of Asia Minor. The sacred island's last notable visitor was the Roman emperor, Hadrian.

Today, only ruins of the sanctuary remain. They are mute, as were the devotees who once sought initiation there; like the other Greek Mysteries – the Eleusinian and Orphic – those of Samothrace were never divulged.

ATHINA KALOGEROPOULOU

Sanctity among the Hellenes : a Postscript

We know what was *sacred* to the Hellenes, but we do not know precisely what they understood by *sanctity* and what it signified to the inner self. We know what ideas and objects were considered to possess the attributes of sanctity; we know the sacred places and religious festivals, as well as the symbols used during these festivals, notably the public celebrations at which participants were not required to undergo any special form of initiation. It is, however, extremely doubtful whether we are entitled to say that we have grasped the nature of the Hellenes' inner experience of sanctity. In terms of Christianity, monotheism has, by making us servants of God, associated sanctity with the timidity of the sinful soul, with human unworthiness. This is one of the factors which inhibit us from grasping what sanctity meant to the Hellenes.

There is, however, another important factor: the Hellenes spoke of religion only with the voice of the poet, philosopher, historian and orator, never with the voice of prophet and priest. The Greek religion had 'no religious books which might convey the deepest meaning and context of the ideas with which the Greek entered into communion with the divine powers, which his faith creates for him' (Erwin Rohde). However, this deficiency also had its good side. If there had been a priesthood which devised a theological system and crystallized it in writing, 'the entire epic poetry [of the Greeks] would have been impossible' (Jacob Burckhardt). The same would have applied to the tragic poetry that derived from Homer, or to fine art in the 'grand manner' and 'beautiful manner', to quote Winckelmann, or to that kind of philosophy which proceeded from the law-giving human mind. The city-state, too, that 'work of art', that most autonomous of all the political entities ever created, would never have existed. Hellas would not have been Hellas.

The poets did not give us the Greek *religion*; they gave us *myth*. Greek poets consummated 'the transition from faith to myth . . . But the gods dwell in faith. They were begotten by faith, attain transformation in and through it, die with it, but can live on as beautiful shades' (Ulrich von Wilamowitz-Moellendorff). These shades – and only they – are what we know.

Thanks to the Hellenes' sculptural impulse, these beautiful shades assumed tangible and visible form. Would we be justified in calling the figures portrayed by Byzantine icons tangible and visible? I doubt it very much. Sanctity is, by its very nature, non-visual. Byzantine painting merely hints at sanctity without rendering it visible. We do not see it, only sense its existence. Zeus, Apollo, Hermes and Aphrodite, by contrast, invited the Hellenes to gaze upon them. Faith – all that inhabited the heart of the Hellenes and was sacred in the religious sense of the word – combined with myth to become poetic and sculptural beauty. Beauty, too, was sacred; likewise friendship and the concept of the city-state. This brings us, however, to another type of sanctity. Although the ethically or aesthetically sacred (sublime) may have been indirectly linked with that which was sacred in the religious sense, it does not lead us to sanctity proper.

The poetic and moral licence with which Homer – and, later, the tragic poets – treated the divine and heroic myths might well prompt us to conclude that the moment at which the Hellenes began to overcome their poetic reticence also signalled their emancipation from a religious sense of sanctity; that they preserved divine worship – respect for that which they called *nenomismena* or *nomima* – solely from force of habit and possibly because it accorded with political or even pan-Hellenic considerations of expediency. I do not think we are entitled to draw such a conclusion. There are, on the contrary, many indications that the Hellenes' religious festivals continued to be important events in their lives, but we cannot tell whether they bore any relation to that which we call sacred in the religious sense.

It may be that Olympus or heaven aroused no sense of sanctity in the Hellenic soul. It is possible that the underworld, Hades, likewise failed to evoke this feeling. What is certain is that, to the Hellenes, the grave was sacred in the religious sense.

It is probable that among all peoples, even those who preserved their religion through revelation, sanctity in its religious essence derived from death and the human wonderment inspired by it. 'It was, perhaps, at the sight of death that man first formed an idea of the supernatural. . . . Death was the first mystery' (Fustel de Coulanges). The Hellenes may have turned first to the earth-gods and later to the Olympian or celestial gods. The earth-gods were originally – before human imagination created the more abstract gods of the underworld – mortal men who had died, dead people whom one had learnt to love and admire as fellow beings. Poetic imagination probably created not only Olympus but Hades as well. No imagination was needed to render the grave visible to the human eye. To the Hellenes, their mortal dead always remained more sacred than the immortal gods. The dead were the undisputed family deities, heroes and spirits. The Athenians accepted the parody of Hades in Aristophanes' *Frogs* as altogether natural, but they would never have tolerated a play which burlesqued the grave. After all, tradition had it that the dead still needed food and clothing; this was immortality in subterranean gloom, not on the heavenly heights.

Could this idea be the key to perception of the substance of sanctity in the Hellenic soul? I think not. It would more probably open the door to error. It is extremely doubtful whether the Hellenes really believed that life continued after death. 'The Greek did . . . everything so as to live on, if only in the memory of his fellow-citizens' (Lessing). Continued existence in the hereafter must have been not only questionable to the Hellenes but, possibly, incomprehensible as well. Poetry shows us men – especially great men – alive after death, but the Hellenic religion, reticent about all that relates to afterlife, is silent on this point too.

But 'non-being [also] forms part of mundane reality', and Hades, like 'the other ancient deities of death, *who guarantee no "survival"*, compel us to observe that the ancient religious outlook, in its unreflecting way, included non-being among the forms of being' (Karl Kerényi). If this consideration holds good, we may possibly discover in it something of the Hellenic sense of sanctity, which is altogether different in quality from that which governs the culture of the Christian West.

In the Christian Church prayers are offered to Almighty God – and in this supplication reposes what is, to us, the moment of supreme sanctity –

to bestow his mercy on mortal sinners: *miserere nobis*. We implore God to forgive the departed (in whose cold and expressionless countenance we recognize ourselves) and take them to his bosom, which encompasses infinity and eternity. This 'creaturely' sentiment would have been alien to the Hellenes, who must have felt something utterly and completely different when confronted by death and the dead, by his own forthcoming non-existence, by this inconceivable vision of another form of being.

We have sufficient grounds for believing that the secret Hellenic festivals, notably the Mysteries of Eleusis, related to this singular experience, the humanly incomprehensible experience of a non-being which is the negation, not only of physical (and mental) existence, but also of the state designated by the word 'nothingness'.

If we could guess the nature of the Eleusinian Mysterium Magnum – and all attempts to come to grips with it have so far failed – we should also be able to discern the true significance of what was sacred in the minds of the Hellenes.

PANAYOTIS KANELLOPOULOS

Practical Suggestions for the Visitor

The following notes outline the various methods of reaching each of the sites discussed, together with other places of interest which can be combined in a single trip. For detailed information about times of trains and buses the local Tourist Police or other information services should be consulted.

MAINLAND SITES (including Peloponnese) easily accessible from Athens:

Amphiareion

Distance from Athens 49 km. (30 miles) by road via Kifiseia, Kapandriti and Kalamos. The site of the battle of Marathon (490 BC) can also be visited by turning off at Kapandriti. See also note on Rhamnus, on p. 205, below.

Argos

Distance from Athens 136 km. (83 miles). A visit by car can also include Epidaurus (see p. 89); the ancient city is reached via Eleusis (see p. 75), Megara, Corinth and Fichtia (where the road to Mycenae turns off). Organized coach tours also combine visits to Argos (see p. 39) and Epidaurus, and more extended tours take in Corinth, Mycenae, etc. The town can be reached from Athens by bus or train, and there is also a bus service between Argos and Epidaurus.

The museum is in the centre of the town, while the archaeological site is on the outskirts (on the road to Tripolis).

Brauron

Distance from Athens 36 km. (22 miles) by the (northern) route to Cape
Sunium; leaving the main road near Markopoulon, the visitor drives
north-eastwards for 8 km. (5 miles) to the site and the new museum
containing finds made there. Also worth visiting in this district are the
numerous Byzantine churches with frescoes.

Delphi

Distance from Athens 167 km. (90 miles); the site can be reached by car
via Daphni, Eleusis (see p. 75), Thebes, Levkadia and Arachova. There
are also regular coach trips (about 4 hours journey) from the capital, and
visitors can either return the same day or spend the night at the Byzantine monastery of Hosios Lukas. Alternatively, two-day tours to Delphi
and Olympia are available, and longer round trips taking in Corinth,
Mycenae, Epidaurus (see p. 89), Olympia (see p. 101) and Delphi.

Delphi can also be reached from Patras, the principal port of the
Pelopponese, which is 57 km. (35 miles) distant; the journey can be made
by rail or coach to Aiyion, ferry across the Gulf of Corinth (about
3 hours) to Itea and thence by bus.

Eleusis

Distance from Athens 23 km. (14 miles); accessible by car, bus or train.
The eleventh-century Byzantine monastery at Daphni is also worth a
visit en route, and this trip (by car) can be extended to include a visit to
Delphi (see p. 59). Alternatively Eleusis may be visited en route to Argos
(see p. 39) and Epidaurus (see p. 89).

Epidaurus

A visit to Epidaurus can be combined with Argos, 42 km. (25 miles)
distant by road, via Tiryns and Nauplia. For visitors without a car,
special coach trips from the capital or bus services from Argos are
available (see p. 39).

Olympia

From Athens regular two-day coach trips to Delphi (see p. 59) and
Olympia are organized. Olympia can also be reached by rail (Athens-

Patras, and from Patras via Pyrgos), and there is a bus service from Patras.

By car—a distance of 100 km. (60 miles)—Pyrgos can be reached from Patras via Lechaina, Andravida and Gastuni; from Pyrgos the road leads eastwards (to Tripolis) a further 22 km. (13 miles). The museum and ruins are on the eastern outskirts of the modern town of Olympia.

Mount Ptoion
Distance from Athens 95 km. (57 miles) accessible by car, taking national highway N1. Just south of the village of Akraiphnion (formerly Karditsa) is the ancient acropolis; the sanctuary of Apollo lies 3.5 km. (2 miles) further on, and is reached on foot.

The principal finds from these sites can be seen in the National Museum in Athens, and in the museum at Thebes.

Rhamnus
Distance from Athens 56 km. (34 miles), via Marathon (see itinerary for Amphiareion, above) and Kato Souli, from which a dusty road leads to the sanctuary of Nemesis.

Sparta
To reach Sparta by car the route to Pyrgos (see itinerary for Olympia, above) should be followed, and thence by either of the two roads (via Olympia or Andritsaina) to Tripolis. From Tripolis, the distance via Selassia to Sparta is 65 km. (39 miles). A detour can be made from Andritsaina to the temple of Apollo at Bassae, 12 km. (7 miles) distant.

Organized day trips by coach are available from Tripolis in summer to Sparta and Mistra.

MAINLAND SITES (Epirus)

The Oracle of the Dead
From the port of Igoumenitsa, the site of the Oracle of the Dead can be reached by road, a distance of 45 km. (28 miles), via Margariti, Kastri to

Kanalakion; from here to the village of Mesapotamon and the confluence of the rivers Cocytus and Acheron is a further 8.5 km. (5 ½ miles).

The site can also be visited from Preveza, by bus via Kanalakion, or direct, a distance of 52.5 km. (33 miles).

Dodona

Dodona, after Delphi the most important oracular shrine, is situated in a narrow valley, 22 km. (13 miles) south of Ioannina, the capital of Epirus. From here the site can be reached by car or bus. Ioannina can likewise be reached by car or bus from the port of Igoumenitsa (to which there is a ferry service from Brindisi in Italy), a distance of 100 km. (60 miles).

ISLAND SITES

Delos

The island of Delos can be reached by boat either from the mainland port of Piraeus or from islands in the Cyclades, e.g. Mykonos, and elsewhere in the Aegean.

Samos

The island can be reached by boat from Piraeus or from various islands in the Aegean. The site of the ancient city of Samos is occupied by the town of Pythagoreion (formerly Tigani); the sanctuary of Hera is 6 km. (3 ½ miles) to the west.

Samothrace

From the port of Salonica, capital of Macedonia, there is a regular service by boat to the island sanctuary of the 'Great Gods'.

Map of Greece and the Aegean

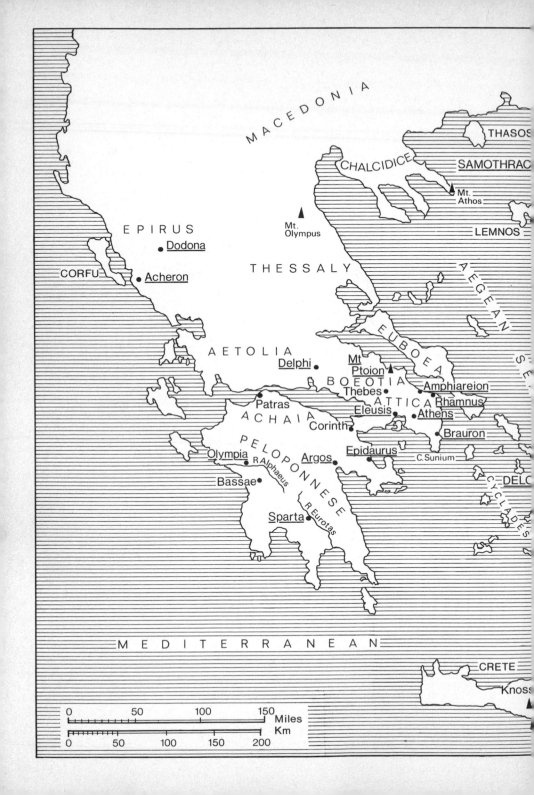

THRACE

PHRYGIA

● Troy

● Pergamum

=SBOS

LYDIA

● Erythrae

HIOS

● Ephesus   R Maeander

SAMOS

KONOS   CARIA

NAXOS

SPORADES

RHODES

S E A

Map of Greece and the
Aegean sea ; sites
discussed are shown
underlined.

List of illustrations

211

Index